The Power of Presumptions

Challenging the Modern Christian Perspective through the Lens of Scripture

Jonathan Lu

Copyright © 2023 by Jonathan Lu.

All rights reserved.

No portion of this book may be reproduced in any form without written permission from the publisher or author, except as permitted by U.S. copyright law.

All Scripture quotations, unless otherwise noted, are taken from the World English Bible.

Scripture quotations marked KJV are taken from the King James Version.

The Bible translations selected for this book are not endorsements from the author.

Contents

Acknowledgments	VII
1. Awaken	1
2. Desiring to Follow Christ	9
3. Finding Joy in Freedom	19
4. Freedom in Christ	25
5. Confronting Church Traditions	35
6. Boasting of Our Weakness	45
7. Prayer and Meditation	55
8. Focusing on Our Speech	61
9. Learning to Listen	69
10. Words of "Good" Intention	77
11. Wholistic Worldview	87
12. Gaining Discernment	97
13. Hidden Temptations	107
14. Fleeing Addictions	117
15. Recognition Vs. Understanding	125
16. Promise Keeper	139

17. "Christian" in Name Alone   147
18. A New Era to Come   155

Acknowledgments

This book would not have been possible without God and the people He surrounded me with. To my best of friends: Josh, Maddy, Bryan, and my wife. Thank you for going above and beyond the call of friendship.

1

Awaken

Wake up! It is time for us, the church, to arise. As Christians, we have been asleep, consumed by laziness and distractions, proud of our own works, a people too proud to lower ourselves onto the ground before the King of kings.

We have blindly followed those who speak from the pulpit, the media, our friends, and our families, while simultaneously stating that God remains first in our lives. We have allowed our presumptions to distort the truth that God showed us in His Word. We have been quick to assert our points and argue our ways rather than quick to listen and slow to speak. Since when was it "me first" rather than "the last shall become first"?

Oftentimes, we, the church body, have ignored our One and Only Groom, prostituting ourselves to win popularity contests and worldly gifts. We point our fingers in every direction and blame others for our every misfortune. But are we willing to point those same fingers back at ourselves and learn from our own mistakes? Are we willing to lower ourselves before the Creator of the universe, or will we continue ignoring the truths shown in Scripture?

For many of us have fallen into despair, wondering if what we believe is true. We question God when things do not go the way we expected. Yet maybe it is those very expectations that cloud our minds. Maybe we have viewed Scripture through the lens of sinful desire rather than God's eyes. Then, as Christians, are we ready to begin by challenging our presumptions and what we think we know? Will we lower ourselves once again before our first Love and choose His ways over our own?

Because no trial, trivial or not, should deter us from Him. But if you will go on this journey with me in search of truth, I hope you are prepared for the bumpy ride and ready for your presumptions to be challenged. For He is worthy. Yet for far too long we have chosen the path of least resistance, and now is the time of change, the time of awakening.

Because if we claim to be "Christians," we should be the ones who truly understand the meaning of such a title. Then, did we know that the journey of following Jesus would not only be hard, but impossible without Him by our side at every moment? For to seek perfection in imperfect bodies, to continue fighting without worldly recognition, and to stand up for what is right even at the cost of our lives may truly seem insane to the world's eyes.

So, as we begin, our first question must be, is God still worth it? For we can presume that we love God, sing hymns and praises at the top of our lungs, and declare ourselves Christ-followers. However, when we look for the actions that should pair with our claims, many times we find barren soil instead of abundant fruit.

We see leaders passionately speaking to their congregations about God, only to later discover they were quietly living in the darkness of sin with no remorse or desire for repentance. We see the church speak so highly of love, family, brotherhood, and sisterhood, yet ignore those same "family members" in their times of need. It is no wonder many of those outside the church view us as hypocrites!

We proclaim boldly that Jesus is the only way to be saved. We affirm John 14:6, which says, "Jesus said to him, 'I am the way, the truth, and the life. No one comes to the Father, except through me.'" We state that we are saved by our faith in Jesus as explained through Ephesians 2:8-9, "For by grace you have been saved through faith, and that not of yourselves; it is the gift of God, not of works, that no one would boast."

But it is easy to make these bold claims without first meditating on what they mean. Because if it is by "faith" in Jesus that we are saved, we must understand what that "faith" entails. Is it just an ordinary faith—the mere belief that God exists and died for us? For even the demons believe those facts, as shown in James 2:19: "You believe that God is one. You do well. The demons also believe, and shudder."

The fact that the demons "believe and shudder" shows that they can even have a better understanding than we do of who God is and the power He has over everything. However, this belief alone is not enough to save because "faith" in Christ is not merely an acknowledgement of facts. So, what then is the definition of "faith" that is required to be saved?

When speaking to the masses, Jesus explained what "faith" in Him means. Luke 14:25-27 says, "Now great multitudes were going with him. He turned and said to them, 'If anyone comes to me, and doesn't disregard his own father, mother, wife, children, brothers, and sisters, yes, and his own life also, he can't be my disciple. Whoever doesn't bear his own cross, and come after me, can't be my disciple.'"

Jesus explained what it means to follow Him, to be a disciple of Christ. He stated that in order to follow Him, our desire for Him must outweigh our love for our closest family members. He showed how we must have a heart mentality with the willingness to give up those dearest to us if need be. This desire for Christ must be so great that we would give up our own lives if He called us to.

It is not about doing works to follow Jesus (Ephesians 2:9) but about having the faith to desire God above all else, to make Him Lord over all in our lives. It is about prostrating ourselves before the King of kings, submitting everything before Him. For He is worthy, regardless of any pain and suffering it may cost.

However, some may shake their heads in disagreement, pointing at Romans 6:23, "For the wages of sin is death, but the free gift of God is eternal life in Christ Jesus our Lord." They may argue that our salvation is a "free gift." But is it possible to claim a gift, even if it is "free," without a willingness to receive it? For if one *refuses* to accept a gift, they *cannot* receive the gift regardless of the price. Therefore, to receive that "free gift" we must have "faith" in Jesus, and in order to have faith in Jesus, we must be willing to be His disciples.

In other words, it is impossible to have "faith" or "receive" Jesus but refuse to follow Him—for this is a complete contradiction. One cannot receive Jesus by running away from Him, and the only way to go to Him is by choosing to become His disciple. Therefore, the faith required to become a disciple of Jesus is the same faith required to be saved.

"Easier said than done," one may state. "To always lower oneself and choose to follow God is too hard," another may argue. To them I say, *wrong*; it is not too hard. It is *impossible*. Within our current sinful bodies, it is impossible to perfectly desire the things God wants for us at every moment. Hence, the decision to follow Jesus, despite the consequences, is only the starting point of our salvation.

6   THE POWER OF PRESUMPTIONS

Jesus illustrated this right after He gave His explanation of the requirements of discipleship, continued in verses 28-30 of Luke 14, "For which of you, desiring to build a tower, doesn't first sit down and count the cost, to see if he has enough to complete it? Or perhaps, when he has laid a foundation, and is not able to finish, everyone who sees begins to mock him, saying, 'This man began to build, and wasn't able to finish.'"

Through this first example, Jesus explains how the decision to follow Him is like counting the materials needed *before* constructing a tower. Likewise, the second parable in verses 31-33 further illustrates that discipleship to Jesus is only the *starting point* by showing a King deciding whether to go into war:

> Or what king, as he goes to encounter another king in war, will not sit down first and consider whether he is able with ten thousand to meet him who comes against him with twenty thousand? Or else, while the other is yet a great way off, he sends an envoy, and asks for conditions of peace. So therefore whoever of you who doesn't renounce all that he has, he can't be my disciple.

In both cases, Jesus describes the decision to follow Him as only a starting point rather than the journey itself. Therefore, we should reevaluate if He is still worth it in our lives before continuing to claim the title of "Christian." For this is not a decision to be made hastily or lightly.

Therefore, are we willing to be ridiculed in front of all for the sake of He who bled for all? Are we willing to lose our closest relationships for the inconvenient truths that may cause strife? Are we willing to lose all our material possessions if He calls us to? Is it worth it to be murdered and tortured for the sake of the gospel? Is Jesus worth it?

Is the Creator of the universe worth it? Is the One who continues to orchestrate every cell in our bodies and gives us life worth it? Is the God who continues to call us back despite our shortcomings, the One who has chosen to love and die for us, worth it? I cannot answer that question for you, but as for me, that answer can only be a resounding and unequivocal "Yes!"

2

Desiring to Follow Christ

Yet even in the decision to follow Jesus, His help is needed. We are shown this through the story of the rich man when he approached Jesus to ask how he could receive eternal life. Matthew 19:16 says, "Behold, one came to him and said, 'Good teacher, what good thing shall I do, that I may have eternal life?'"

In response to the rich man's question, in verses 21-22, "Jesus said to him, 'If you want to be perfect, go, sell what you have, and give to the poor, and you will have treasure in heaven; and come, follow me.' But when the young man heard the saying, he went away sad, for he was one who had great possessions."

In this passage, Jesus shows again that salvation requires that a person desire God above all else. By telling the rich man to "go sell what you have," Jesus challenged the man's heart by asking if he was willing to give up everything to follow Him, including all his material possessions.

We can know this because verse 21 shows that if the man had done so, his reward would have been "treasure in heaven." Jesus clarified the reward once more in verse 23 by using the words "enter into the Kingdom of Heaven." Therefore, through these interactions, we can see the importance of having the willingness to follow God no matter the cost.

However, we cannot accomplish this decision alone. For after this encounter with the rich young man, Jesus explained to His disciples the difficulty of making that choice in Matthew 19:23-26:

> Jesus said to his disciples, "Most certainly I say to you, a rich man will enter into the Kingdom of Heaven with difficulty. Again I tell you, it is easier for a camel to go through a needle's eye, than for a rich man to enter into the Kingdom of God." When the disciples heard it, they were exceedingly astonished, saying, "Who then can be saved?" Looking at them, Jesus said, "With men this is impossible, but with God all things are possible."

Some may argue that Jesus was only speaking about those who are "rich," but this interpretation is problematic. For even the disciples themselves quickly realized that Jesus was speaking about everyone, remarking, "Who then can be saved?"

Therefore, by stating, "With men this is impossible," Jesus explained how it is impossible for all, not just rich men, to be saved in our own strength. For all fall short of the glory of God (Romans 3:23). He further illustrated this statement with the visual example of a camel going through the eye of a needle, a task that is obviously impossible. Yet, as He elaborated in verse 26, while this is an impossible task for man, it is still possible through God.

In other words, even the simple decision of choosing to follow Jesus is an impossible task without God. It is only by His tremendous grace and mercy that we can have our eyes opened and follow Him, regardless of the cost.

Then, is it possible that we have forgotten what it means to be loved by the Lord? Because it is easy to forget who gave us our first desires for Jesus to begin with. Thankfully though, 1 John 4:19 reminds us we can only love God because He loved us first, "We love him, because he first loved us."

Then, how did I fall in love with God? Did I love God first, or did He love me first? Reflecting back, the question of love always felt incomplete. While growing up within the church, I was mocked and ridiculed for my shortcomings, belittled by those who called themselves Christians. I allowed the words of others to grow and fester in my heart, bringing me down into a life of self-pity.

My callousness grew as I was constantly told that my best was never enough and received little praise. I found no meaning or purpose in life as I progressed through the years. Day and night, my only plea was to hear God's voice. Desperately seeking a sense of purpose and drive, I sought to know whether this life was only coincidence. Yet, the silence continued, and it seemed like an eternity would pass, until one day.

For I had presumed that I knew what it meant for God to love me, but I was ignorant of what His love really meant. I had always heard that Jesus loves us. I heard that our freedom came at a price and that we all fall short of God's expectations of perfection. As Romans 3:23 says, "For all have sinned, and fall short of the glory of God."

I knew that the price for our sin was death (Romans 6:23) but that God loves us despite our sinfulness and failures. Romans 5:8 says, "But God commends his own love toward us, in that while we were yet sinners, Christ died for us."

I was told repeatedly of the grace and mercy that God had for us when taking our sins upon Himself on the cross. Yet, what did it mean for God to love me? Why should I follow Him while knowing the cost? What did it mean for Jesus to pay the price for my sins? These were the questions that constantly plagued my mind.

However, little did I know that the answer to my prayers and questions would soon be revealed. For on one particular day, I planned to purchase over thirty Bibles and a supply of canned foods to keep in the back of my car. I made this weird decision the previous night after being convicted of the personal excuses I made for myself. God convicted me of my selfishness and greed that prevented me from giving to complete strangers and those in need.

God reminded me that Christians should be "cheerful givers" through 2 Corinthians 9:6-7, which says, "Remember this: he who sows sparingly will also reap sparingly. He who sows bountifully will also reap bountifully. Let each man give according as he has determined in his heart; not grudgingly, or under compulsion; for God loves a cheerful giver."

Yet too long had I made excuses about how I had nothing to give when approached by random people. So, I decided to give despite my financial status and share the gospel regardless of any situation.

But on this day, before leaving to purchase the items on my list, I had reservations about going to the bookstore. My sinful nature desired otherwise because it was raining. The water poured down like a waterfall. Yet, I continued onward. As I drove half-heartedly to the store and approached the nearby parking spot, I realized I had forgotten to bring an umbrella.

Out of my selfish desire to remain dry, I quickly prayed, "God, please make the rain stop because I do not want to be soaking wet when walking to the store." As I finished praying, the most interesting thing happened: at that very moment, the downpour vanished.

I quickly chuckled to myself and rushed inside to purchase the Bibles. With a wide smile from one cheek to the other, I checked out with books in hand. As I left, I heard the cashier remark, "God is good," but this statement left my mind as quickly as I had heard it, for it was now time to move on to the next location. I still needed to drive to the grocery store to purchase the canned goods.

However, while driving to the next destination, again I prayed out of my selfishness, "Lord, if possible, please have the canned goods be on sale as well." For at that time, I was still just a poor student with little money, and I did not wish to deplete what little I had saved. Yet, I had no real expectation for them to be on sale.

Because during this time, this grocery store rarely had any sales. Approximately twice a year, they would bring down the price of these specific canned goods from what normally sold for a single dollar to eighty-eight cents each. Therefore, it seemed unlikely that they would be on sale.

Yet, as I walked closer to the canned goods aisle, any small expectation of an answered prayer completely vanished because I soon realized that very few items were actually on sale. Finally, I arrived at the spot where the cans I planned to purchase were located.

Shockingly, a sudden burst of uncontrolled laughter quickly came upon me. For the cans were not on their biannual sale of eighty-eight cents—instead, they had a special sale that day, which I have never witnessed again after. They were being sold for the unheard-of price of sixty-three cents each.

While continuing in my joy, I probably seemed like a madman to those around me. I began placing cans on top of cans into my shopping cart until I filled it to the brim. With an ever-widening smile, my laughter carried on all the way through the checkout line and even while packing the cans into the car.

However, as I drove away from the store, my laughter quickly subsided. As I approached a stoplight, an unceasing stream of tears now replaced my laughter. For it was here that I had a realization.

I realized God had been listening to my prayers the entire time. I realized God had continued to listen to me, even though I prayed from selfish desires. It was here that I remembered those simple words from the book clerk: "God is good." In this moment, for the first time in my life, I finally understood what it meant for God to love me.

I had a realization deep down inside that it was not just three simple words, "God loves you," but that God loves "me." As in, God was willing to listen to "me," to speak with "me," to spend time with "me," to put up with "me." I realized that I was not just another number, but an actual person to Him; the Creator of the universe knew who I was.

It finally struck home in my heart of hearts and broke me as a person. But who was I? Why would God listen to my selfish requests? Why did God love me? It was hard enough for others to like me, let alone love me. I did not even like "me." I was no one.

Why would God love someone like me? I was just a dirty, hate-filled liar. Why would He want me? Why? And it was as if God just spoke to me, "Because I chose you." "I crafted you." "I paid the ultimate price for you." "Because I love you."

On that day, I heard His call. It was there in that moment that I realized what it meant for God to love me. It was His overabundant love that made me realize He is worth it. He is worth the sacrifice of all our worldly desires and pleasures because my God even gave me the desire for Him, the desire to follow Him no matter the cost.

He gave me a new purpose and drive, opening my eyes to the self-destructive nature of my sinfulness, revealing intentionality behind this world, and showing me what true love is. He showed me it was a personal relationship and that God did not just love everyone broadly, but that He loved me individually.

He even gave me a new heart that helped me to begin caring deeply for those around me, an attribute that I had severely lacked previously. He became as real to me as my physical family. I could not read enough of the Scriptures to quench this new thirst and hunger for God. I needed everyone to know who this God was that changed me, and I wept for those who did not know Him. From death to life is the only way to describe the feeling.

Likewise, God loves us even though we are dirty. Even with our failings, misgivings, and short-comings, God continues to desire us to come home. For He took the price of the old sacrificial system that could only temporarily cover our sins. He took our sins upon Himself—past, present, and future (Hebrews 10:8-12).

He was crucified on the cross and resurrected for us. He took all of that pain and suffering for you and me. He then became the ultimate payment for all of our sins. John 3:16 says, "For God so loved the world, that he gave his one and only Son, that whoever believes in him should not perish, but have eternal life."

Yet, the fight against sin is no simple matter. As stated previously, it is an impossible task for us in these current mortal bodies. Therefore, in every moment, sin remains a painful reminder that we will never reach perfection in this incomplete world, but it also reminds us how great the mercy and grace of God is.

Likewise, only through the tremendous grace and mercy of God have we been born anew, redeemed of our sins and lifelessness. And though that initial feeling of love toward God may feel like it will never fade, the inner struggles from within us will continue to persist. In between the Holy Spirit and our old selves, a great battle continues to wage on.

3

Finding Joy in Freedom

Many times, I have given up only to be shown the vastness of God's love for me. The farther I walked down the path of righteousness, the more my eyes trembled at the sight of just how wide the chasm between perfection and imperfection was. I saw a chasm so deep that even the dark despaired. It was a chasm so vast the end was nowhere in sight. None could cross, except through a holy, perfect, and loving God through His sacrifice for us. Yet, to stop struggling against sinful urges and desires would make light of His sacrifice.

Eventually, though, even the strongest of feelings can subside from within. This happened to me as well. The honeymoon period passed. With butterflies stolen and jadedness in their place, I returned to brutal reality. The years of overwhelming trials, temptations, and never-ending spiritual warfare took its toll on me.

I was faced with the frustrations of my own failures and of my current situation. At this point in time, I had just graduated from seminary, and I was currently involved with a local church. It felt wonderful to be recognized and praised by others while leading various groups. Yet, that feeling of happiness soon departed when God called me to another church.

Through many months of prayer and counsel from my fellow brothers in Christ, they agreed that this was indeed a calling from the Lord, but my heart became distraught as the time approached for me to leave. For this new calling was to a church very well known to me. It was the same place where I had once been traumatized as a child. It was a place that I did not wish to go back to. It was my home church that I was now called to, the place that I had grown up.

But I did not wish to go against my God's calling. So, I quickly rejected any other job offers I had previously received and returned to my home church. As I arrived, it became just as I had feared. The church leaders there cared little for my return. They did not give me any responsibility when returning. Instead, I was met with apathy and indifference. Yet still I had faith in my Lord and in His calling.

I volunteered myself where I could, giving all my time and effort. However, my sinful nature continued to reveal itself. Frustrations mounted as the years passed, eventually consuming me. I became more and more weary with little-to-no recognition from church leaders, and I fell further into despair.

I spent many nights pleading with the Lord, pleading to be free. I wanted to be free from the shackles that bound my feet from leaving that church. For the additional conflicts that arose continued to stack like weights upon my back. However, this plea would get no response other than the continued silence of the blowing winds.

Besides volunteering my time at the church, I needed to provide for my family. Therefore, I spent all my time between work and church, leaving no time for rest. This only worsened my mental health. The physical toil of the odd jobs added further to my distress. I felt burdened with more than I could handle.

Eventually, as I began another day at my paid job, I unraveled. Sweat poured down my face as I cleaned the many floor-to-ceiling windows once again. I felt like I was being taken advantage of by my coworkers, who claimed that it was because of my height that I needed to do the job. It felt as if I had wasted years of my life, and in my heart, I told the Lord that I was done. I had continued in silence long enough, and I saw no end.

I was finally finished. Filled with feelings of resentment and anger, I had reached my limit. For even though I remembered John 6:13, that we would have tremendous hardships while in this world as Christians, I felt like an unbearable burden had overtaken me. It felt as if there were more burdens than just the regular burdens of being a Christ-follower. It felt like I was drowning.

Yet, in the same moment I hit my limit, God finally spoke. He reminded me of Matthew 11:28-30: "Come to me, all you who labor and are heavily burdened, and I will give you rest. Take my yoke upon you, and learn from me, for I am gentle and lowly in heart; and you will find rest for your souls. For my yoke is easy, and my burden is light."

God reminded me that His yoke was supposed to be light, that being attached to the Lord was not supposed to be difficult. This made me think back on my own life. I questioned why the load on my back felt so heavy for the past years and quickly realized it was me. I was the one who had caused the extra burdens!

I thought back on how God called me to go to that church, and while that remained true even then, I realized God did not explicitly tell me anything else. He did not promise me a title or recognition. I was the one who desired those things. He did not tell me how I should go about being a part of that church or what other jobs I should take. I was the one who decided to work those specific jobs. It was all self-caused! If I wanted, I could quit—even at that very moment!

God did not bind me to that job, nor did I have to place extra burdens upon myself. Working myself to death and volunteering at every opportunity was my own choice. Therefore, I had the freedom to stop. It felt as if all the weight that I had previously placed on my back vanished.

Laughter quickly ensued as I continued my workday. I decided to continue working that job; however, my previous frustrations were now replaced with a sense of joy. This joy was created through a mentality shift that made me realize I had more freedom than I had first thought, that God may sometimes remain silent in His responses to give us space within the parameters He already placed. I realized I was free as long as I remained within the guidelines that God placed in my life. I no longer felt like chains were binding me, rather, I felt like I was in a field of freedom enclosed by a hedge of protection.

Then, this leads us to the question: What does it mean to be "free" as Christians? This term "freedom" has been used frequently but rarely correctly. Many have used this term to mean "to do as one pleases," while others have used it as a scapegoat to ignore Old Testament laws. But is this what it means to be free?

4

Freedom in Christ

In Romans 6:18, the apostle Paul explains we are now free from sin: "Being made free from sin, you became bondservants of righteousness." However, in Galatians 3, he goes over in depth what it means to be "free" from those sins.

He explains that our freedom and salvation were not because of following laws or rules, but because of our faith in Christ Jesus, our faith to follow Him no matter the cost. In Galatians 3:2-3, Paul wrote, "I just want to learn this from you. Did you receive the Spirit by the works of the law, or by hearing of faith? Are you so foolish? Having begun in the Spirit, are you now completed in the flesh?"

Then, he continued to further explain how the laws of the Old Testament were not pointless, rather they were tools that God used. They were the "tutor" that helped teach God's people of their own failures and sinfulness before the physical arrival of Jesus. In Galatians 3:24, he wrote, "So that the law has become our tutor to bring us to Christ, that we might be justified by faith."

Therefore, the Old Testament laws were tutors and guideposts in place of the Holy Spirit before He could dwell within us and become our ultimate guide as shown in John 16:13: "However when he, the Spirit of truth, has come, he will guide you into all truth, for he will not speak from himself; but whatever he hears, he will speak. He will declare to you things that are coming."

Many seem to think that just because we are now free from the laws of old, we can ignore them. However, this is not the case at all because those Old Testament laws were guides! Do guideposts on a nature trail lose all meaning when we do not have to follow them? Surely not! We can, of course, choose to wander off the beaten path and still arrive at the intended finish line, but that does not mean the guideposts have no use anymore. For if we get lost, we can still use them to find our way back onto the path.

Likewise, it means that these same Old Testament laws still have meaning as a concurrent guide even today. Because even though we have freedom from performing the laws of old, it was these very laws that God Himself placed to guide the Israelites.

Therefore, even though the Holy Spirit now lives within us (1 Corinthians 3:16), having become our ultimate teacher and guidepost (John 16:13), those Old Testament laws are still helpful for us today in helping discern our Lord's will because God created those laws with the purpose of guiding people to righteousness.

So, rather than just ignore the laws of old, we should instead find out the reasons God placed them there to begin with. How did they help guide the Israelites in righteousness? How can they help guide us currently? Because in the same manner they helped in the past, they still have a use in discerning God's voice today.

This then leads us to another important question. Why are we free from the laws of old? Besides the obvious answer that Jesus paid the price on the cross, why exactly are we free from the same laws God Himself placed on His people to begin with?

We are free from the old laws because the laws themselves never had any power. Just as a knife can help sculpt beautifully crafted artwork or be used to hurt another, a tool is nothing more than a tool without the wielder. Likewise, we are free from the laws because it was never the laws themselves that caused our sinfulness. Instead, it was always about the heart mentalities behind why we follow or ignore those rules that caused our actions to be evil. Jesus showcased these exact reasons when He talked about sin.

He explained how hating your brother is equivalent to murder in Matthew 5:21-22:

> You have heard that it was said to the ancient ones, "You shall not murder;" and "Whoever shall murder shall be in danger of the judgment." But I tell you, that everyone who is angry with his brother without a cause shall be in danger of the judgment; and whoever shall say to his brother, "Raca!" shall be in danger of the council; and whoever shall say, "You fool!" shall be in danger of the fire of Gehenna.

He explained how lusting after another that is not your spouse is the same as committing adultery in Matthew 5:27-30: "You have heard that it was said, 'You shall not commit adultery;' but I tell you that everyone who gazes at a woman to lust after her has committed adultery with her already in his heart."

And if that was not proof enough, in Matthew 15:19-20 Jesus states plainly, "For out of the heart come forth evil thoughts, murders, adulteries, sexual sins, thefts, false testimony, and blasphemies. These are the things which defile the man; but to eat with unwashed hands doesn't defile the man."

In other words, our sins are due to the heart conditions behind our actions rather than the actions themselves. Why is this important though? This differentiation is important because it explains why we are free from the laws of the Old Testament. It was never about following the rules themselves, instead it was about having the correct heart mentality behind those actions.

It is the same reason why the action of killing a person could be sinful in one case but the right thing to do in another situation. Murdering another out of hatred toward them would be sinful (Matthew 5:21-22). However, a death resulting from defending one's home from wickedness could be the right choice. Because as shown by God's law to the Israelites, Exodus 22:2 excused the defender from guilt: "If the thief is found breaking in, and is struck so that he dies, there shall be no guilt of bloodshed for him"

It has never been about the specific act of killing someone but rather the heart mentality behind the action. Was it being done because it was the just and righteous thing to do, or was it out of our own sin-filled hatred and self-centeredness?

Another good example lies within Romans 14:1-3: "Now accept one who is weak in faith, but not for disputes over opinions. One man has faith to eat all things, but he who is weak eats only vegetables. Don't let him who eats despise him who doesn't eat. Don't let him who doesn't eat judge him who eats, for God has accepted him."

In this passage, the apostle Paul again explained what it means to have "freedom" in Christ. Paul described that the Christian who is not tempted and understands that they can consume anything, including meat, is the stronger person. This is because they understand it is not the action of eating meat itself that is sinful, but the heart mentality behind why they eat it. Despite this, many would bring up this passage to argue that the main point of Paul's message is the right to eat certain meats. Yet, this is not the focus of the passage. How can we know this?

We can know this because in the verses following his talk of eating meat, Paul gave a further example. He spoke of one man valuing one day over another but stated that no matter the day we set aside to honor God, we should do it for the Lord. In Romans 14:5, he wrote, "One man esteems one day as more important. Another esteems every day alike. Let each man be fully assured in his own mind."

Then in verses 6 through 9, he completes his argument for freedom by summarizing his previous examples, showing we can do anything as long as it is for the Lord:

> He who observes the day, observes it to the Lord; and he who does not observe the day, to the Lord he does not observe it. He who eats, eats to the Lord, for he gives God thanks. He who doesn't eat, to the Lord he doesn't eat, and gives God thanks. For none of us lives to himself, and none dies to himself. For if we live, we live to the Lord. Or if we die, we die to the Lord. If therefore we live or die, we are the Lord's. For to this end Christ died, rose, and

lived again, that he might be Lord of both the dead and the living.

Therefore, it matters very little whether or not we choose to partake in certain actions, for every action can be done for the Lord. The correct decision stems from having the correct heart mentality in obedience to Christ.

Hence, in an opposite scenario, if one felt led by God to abstain from eating meat yet continued to partake in their hardness of heart and ignored His call, they would be in sin. The decision to consume the meat would have stemmed from a selfish desire to please oneself rather than a desire to be pleasing to the Lord.

In summary, the action itself has never been the problem. It has always been about whether we are doing it for the right reasons: ourselves or God. Therefore, we have the freedom to watch all movies, play all games, wear any clothing, go to any place, and eat any food or drink.

However, the greater question should not be about whether we *can* do an action but whether we *should*. For as Christ-followers, we are called to not only understand our freedoms in Christ but to be prepared as well, willing to sacrifice those very freedoms for the glorification of God Almighty and our love for others.

For just as we have the freedom to do every action, we are also free to forfeit those very freedoms. Let us not pretend that all actions are equal, as if some acts are not inherently more dangerous than others.

Let us not delude ourselves into the misguided belief that our own ways of life remain justified in our freedom. To give an extreme example, a person lacking sexual temptations *could* watch pornographic materials and remain free from sin, perhaps after being called by God to find sex trafficking victims or to protect others from viewing it. But rare examples of how things *can* be done for good do not automatically mean we *should* do those things. For we all know that pornography has far greater potential to tempt one into sin than lead to spiritual betterment.

Many times, we try to justify our sinful behaviors by arguing that the Bible allows us the freedom to do all actions, whether it be drinking alcohol, tithing, divorce, watching certain movies, or playing specific games. However, it has never been about us following rules blindly but about how we can place God first and foremost in our lives, constructing guardrails to protect us from ourselves and making wise choices to glorify Him. It has never been about what we *can* do but about what we *should* do.

This is the same reason that Paul clearly shows that the right thing to do as Christ-followers is to abstain from all actions that may cause another to stumble in their walk with God in Romans 14:20-21, "Don't overthrow God's work for food's sake. All things indeed are clean, however it is evil for that man who creates a stumbling block by eating. It is good to not eat meat, drink wine, nor do anything by which your brother stumbles, is offended, or is made weak."

Therefore, how can we now selfishly do as we please if we have already decided to follow Christ, knowing the cost? Does our freedom, which stems from God's sacrifice on the cross, mean we should do anything our sinful hearts desire because we have been freed from the bondage of the law? Of course not!

For it is impossible to deceive the Holy Spirit. We either wholeheartedly made the decision to follow Jesus or we did not. Or, as Paul said in Romans 6:1-2, "What shall we say then? Shall we continue in sin, that grace may abound? May it never be! We who died to sin, how could we live in it any longer?"

5

Confronting Church Traditions

At this point, some may have taken interest with this conversation but also wondered, "Why is this such a big deal? Why does it really matter if we understand our freedom in Christ?" The reason is because one of the greatest failures of the church, our failure, is how we have misidentified sinful heart mentalities. We treat actions as if they automatically represent the desires of the heart.

We have forgotten that correlation is not the same as causation. While we can certainly understand that actions stem from the heart and are connected with each other, we must also recognize that specific actions do not always equate to an assumed heart mentality. For practices designed to combat sinful desires do not automatically equate to one having the correct heart mentality, and these distortions have created blind spots in our walks with Christ.

Our false presumptions of what sinful heart mentalities are have led us to become blind followers of men and their rules rather than of God Himself. We have refused to challenge our own preconceived definitions of sin. We have begun to argue our ways over His ways instead of creating mindsets rooted in Scripture.

Whether or not this has been a deliberate act is up for debate. However, we have begun to use the Bible not as a guide to help us think through our actions but as a tool to promote our own agendas!

If we do not care to admit this, then let us consider why we enforce certain spiritual practices over others if the purpose of those practices is to help others grow in Christ. Have we meditated enough on the negative effects of our practices when pushed on others? What is the wisdom of embracing such practices? Have we forgotten to speak with the Lord first before speaking in His place?

May we be reminded of Romans 14:13, which says that we should not place stumbling blocks in front of our brothers and sisters in Christ: "Therefore let's not judge one another any more, but judge this rather, that no man put a stumbling block in his brother's way, or an occasion for falling."

Then is it not a stumbling block for us to present man-made rules and laws that argue our ways while disregarding the counterarguments rooted in Scripture? Do we create new laws to teach one biblical principle at the expense of another? If not, then let me continue to challenge and ask, why do most of us allow politics to dictate which side we align with?

We tell others: left or right. We teach whom to align with politically. We draw a line through the sand and divide ourselves on either side depending on the specific laws we claim to believe in. We talk about the pros and cons of the laws that each candidate may represent, explaining how those laws are about protecting others, protecting nature, or protecting one's freedoms and finances. But why should it matter whether we prefer one law over another?

As previously established, we can do both actions and laws in sin or in righteousness. Just as there were occasions when God told His people to store up food and grain for hard times, there were also moments when the Lord told His people to rely on Him and not hoard food. Just as God told Joseph to store up grain for the coming famine in Genesis 41:47-49, God also ordered His people not to store the manna from heaven that He provided when the Israelites wandered through the desert in Exodus 16:19.

Therefore, whether or not one should prepare food for the future matters little. What matters is the heart mentality. It is about why we do it. Are we doing it for the Lord or ourselves? For our best actions by themselves are like dirty rags, polluted garments before the Lord. Isaiah 64:6 says, "For we have all become as one who is unclean, and all our righteousness is as a polluted garment: and we all fade as a leaf; and our iniquities, like the wind, take us away."

Then what difference is there between laws and actions? For it is not by following laws but due to our faith in God alone that our works are counted as righteousness. Galatians 3:5-6 affirms this, saying, "He therefore who supplies the Spirit to you, and works miracles among you, does he do it by the works of the law, or by hearing of faith? Even as Abraham 'believed God, and it was counted to him for righteousness.'"

Then what are laws but mere tools with no power in themselves? They can be used as shields to protect and provide for their people, or as weapons of destruction that benefit and promote those in power at the expense of all. They can even be ignored altogether.

So why do we teach others to choose between the lesser of two evils? Why do we turn our gaze away from the ones who create and use the laws, pretending as if these very laws dictate godliness rather than the people behind them?

We are told by these same political leaders that we should get vengeance when Jesus told us instead to turn the other cheek in Matthew 5:38-39. They tell us to be proud of ourselves and our accomplishments when the Scriptures proclaim that our arrogance is an abomination and our pride comes before our fall (Proverbs 16:5, 18). They tell us we should take what we desire, while the Ten Commandments teach us not to covet and steal (Exodus 20:15-17).

They claim they are of God while simultaneously regurgitating the lies of Satan. Yet if that is the case, then why do we focus on the law, forgetting about those behind the law, forgetting about patience, gentleness, and self-control (Galatians 5:22-24)? Because it is Jesus who tells us that we can discern the lies of false prophets by their fruits in Matthew 7:15-20.

As Ephesians 6:12 describes, our war is not with man but is spiritual in nature: "For our wrestling is not against flesh and blood, but against the principalities, against the powers, against the world's rulers of the darkness of this age, and against the spiritual forces of wickedness in the heavenly places."

Have we started turning into the Pharisees of old, requiring rules made by man to puff ourselves up? We must ask this because the Pharisees were those who proclaimed their own righteousness over others for following their man-made rules.

If not, then why did we see these man-made laws on full display in churches during the Covid-19 pandemic? Why did many create man-made laws using biblical arguments to proclaim their own righteousness while placing stumbling blocks in front of others? Why did they require people to wear medical face masks within the church? Standing high and mighty, they boasted of their own understanding of Scripture, giving examples of why everyone must follow the laws of the government, and continued to tell their congregations that those who followed their newly created rule are the righteous ones.

They proclaimed that Jesus said to give to Caesar what is Caesar's in Mark 12:17. They said that because the governing bodies order us to wear masks, everyone should simply obey without questioning their authority because of Romans 13:1-2, "Let every soul be in subjection to the higher authorities, for there is no authority except from God, and those who exist are ordained by God. Therefore he who resists the authority, withstands the ordinance of God; and those who withstand will receive to themselves judgment."

But let's not forget that when told by the governing bodies to not teach in the name of "Jesus," the apostles proclaimed they would rather obey God than man in Acts 5:29: "But Peter and the apostles answered, 'We must obey God rather than men.'"

Likewise, the apostles could have argued in favor of that very law, stating that it would still be possible to share the gospel without specifically saying the name "Jesus." However, they chose not to because they determined that this man-made law was not beneficial to follow as a disciple of Christ.

Then, in the present day, where people ignore facts and deny the existence of God, is it not possible that those very people have created laws in accordance with Satan, designed to turn us against our Lord, the very definition of truth itself?

Are we not also called to proclaim against the fear of death, persecution, and disease? As 2 Timothy 1:7 says, "For God didn't give us a spirit of fear, but of power, love, and self-control." Then how does the law of wearing face masks help guide us toward fearlessness? Does it not instead guide us further into fear of death and disease? Why do we treat the statistical likelihood of death as being equivalent to our Lord's will? Did the lepers and the sick get healed by chance and coincidence?

Consider the statistical likelihood of the world being flooded and Noah being saved. Do we believe in chance or a purpose-filled God? Let us not forget that our God is the ultimate authority—not our practices. For He is the One who works everything in accordance to His purpose, as stated in Romans 8:28: "We know that all things work together for good for those who love God, to those who are called according to his purpose."

Another explanation many gave for why they required the wearing of face masks was because we should love our neighbors by thinking about their illnesses and wants. However, doesn't this law also simultaneously refute this same argument by teaching us to ignore the illnesses and wishes of those that contradict that stance? Are we to only love those that side with our ideas and ignore the ones who contradict us?

Is not standing firm in either position a prime cause to create stumbling blocks for our fellow Christians, teaching them to disregard what our Lord has told them? Does it not cause those who have been called by God to sway one way or another to then question and ignore that same calling? Regardless of the pros and cons of wearing face coverings, are we not all brothers and sisters in Christ, even in the disagreement of simple matters?

Yet, there are also times when we may take further steps down the road of our own pride. By frequently making new rules with little to no reasonings rooted in Scripture, we can become just as the Pharisees (Matthew 23:5). One example is how some churches enforce wearing dress clothes to come into the church building. They tell others it is because we should wish to glorify God by wearing our best. However, may I ask where this defense lies within Scripture?

Should we be reminded of 1 Timothy 2:9, which says that women are to adorn themselves with modest apparel, not with jewelry and costly things: "In like manner also, that women adorn themselves in modest apparel, with shamefacedness and sobriety; not with broided hair, or gold, or pearls, or costly array" (KJV)?

Consider what purpose the act of dressing modestly serves. Why should women not wear jewelry and costly apparel? Is not the main reason to prevent one from being puffed up? Then, does this not also apply to us all and not just toward females?

In other words, Scripture does address the clothing we wear in church. It speaks about how clothes can puff us up and explains that we should dress modestly to avoid placing stumbling blocks in front of others.

Then, why do some of us tell others they must wear dress clothes instead of just being modest? Are not dress clothes designed to impress others by nature? Are they not a sign of those with much, rather than those without? If so, then how is this man-made law spiritually beneficial to others when it has a much greater likelihood to puff up rather than humble?

For there is a far greater argument that this rule has more potential to push people further from the Lord. By implying to others that God desires us because of our clothes, we can end up priding ourselves on what we wear rather than being humbled before the Lord. And our goal should not be to create environments designed to make us seem better than others.

Just as the Pharisees of old, we often continue to act as if only the side that agrees with us is correct, while vilifying the opposing side. Are we not all sinners? Do we not all have varying convictions about God? Let us not forget, first and foremost, that we are one body in Christ. Just as one may believe in eating meat and another may be against it, we are each called to different convictions in our walks with Christ. This does not make one better or worse than the other.

Yet, how can we become like the Pharisees? Is it the laws themselves that are to blame? For, as stated earlier, we are free in Christ. Therefore, just as we are free from the law, we also have the freedom to enforce any practice or law. Then what causes our laws to be harmful instead of helpful in guiding others to righteousness? Rather than the law itself being the problem, it is how and why we implement the law. It is our hearts behind why and how we enforce the law that is the issue.

6

Boasting of Our Weakness

What can cause us to create environments that fail to promote a desire for God? It is our sinful heart mentality. And one of the greatest culprits to why our laws can become hindrances and stumbling blocks for others is our pride.

Our pride is what can fool us to believe we should strive between the lesser of two evils, that we should pick laws based on merit alone, that we should decide between socialism or capitalism, and that our actions without God are what have power to change things for the better. This self-pride is what Satan uses to deceive us.

We can foolishly believe that righteousness prevails through the law rather than through God. Yet, it is within these tiny misconceptions that our views of Scripture are contaminated. For we are weak, a people filled with pride who are constantly trying to undermine the grace and mercies of our Lord.

It is that prideful nature that leads us to misunderstand God's grace and mercy, forgetting that only God can transform our actions for righteousness—not the other way around. It causes us to proclaim that we are strong despite Scripture proclaiming the weak are made strong (2 Corinthians 12:9-10). Our pride is what leads us to believe that life has meaning without the Life-Giver.

Because while we talk of our need for salvation and our sinful nature, many times our genuine belief is that God is of no importance. We believe that our laws or actions alone are what cause lasting change in this world. We look at our own accomplishments and think to ourselves, "My self-discipline did that. I did that." Intentionally or unintentionally, our false beliefs have led us to fall into a trap. By believing we can accomplish anything through our power and rules alone, we have become deceived by Satan.

If the Holy Spirit does not lead our actions, then we have taken His place for ourselves. By teaching others that they must follow our rules to follow Jesus, we impose our practices on others. Yet, when did we start believing that laws and practices can heal without the Healer? Instead, we should realize the vanity behind fleshly accomplishments. For through our power alone, who can truly be saved (Isaiah 43:11), and who can fully conquer sin (1 Peter 3:18)?

How, then, has this sinful mentality rooted itself within us? It is because, deep down, we have viewed ourselves as the ones with power. We have removed God, the source of our power, and wrongly believed that our actions have meaning apart from Him. In James 4:10, we are clearly told to address the pride within ourselves: "Humble yourselves in the sight of the Lord, and he will exalt you."

The word "humble" in the Greek is "tapeinoó," meaning to bring low or to humiliate oneself. Have we ever wondered why, throughout Scripture, we are told of the dangers of our pride and that we need to lower ourselves?

Consider why we are told only to give out of a cheerful heart according to 2 Corinthians 9:7. Does God require our money? Who created the trees, the oceans, and the items we cherish? Did we form the earth? Let us not forget that it is God Himself who creates and gives everything, including our most cherished valuables (Colossians 1:16). Then what is the purpose of our giving?

The action of giving is not what has the power for good. Our decision to give is for our benefit rather than the Lord's. It helps us keep joyful hearts even when we have little, focus our attention on the Lord, and prevent our mental enslavement to material goods.

Have we forgotten that God considers even our best deeds dirty (Isaiah 64:6)? Have we forgotten that it is not through our deeds that we are justified and made alive again? For it is only through God that our actions can even be counted righteous, as explained in Romans 4:2-3, "For if Abraham was justified by works, he has something to boast about, but not toward God. For what does the Scripture say? 'Abraham believed God, and it was accounted to him for righteousness.'"

Then why is it we sometimes believe that our actions alone are what have let the Lord down? Since when were we holding Him up? Even if we were to repair a person's body, will they not still eventually perish? If we build a house with our bare hands, will it not someday begin to crumble? Will not the sun eventually set permanently despite our best actions? Does anything have meaning apart from the Lord (Ecclesiastes 1)? Certainly not!

Therefore, our deeds and actions have no meaning outside of the Lord. Our deeds can only be accounted to us as righteousness through the power and grace of our Savior. For it is only through God that our actions can have any meaning behind them.

Our power stems from Christ alone. He is the One who victoriously defeated death and paid for our sins on the cross (1 Corinthians 15:54-57). Yet by believing falsely that we have the power to do anything by ourselves, we have removed the source of our strength. We have forgotten that we are not the sole reason for true success. Our incorrect presumptions have led us to believe that our practices and laws changed us when it was God Himself who changed us, as He is able to use everything for our good (Romans 8:28).

Therefore, our pride can distort our inherent beliefs. Yet how does this sinfulness continue to deceive us? It is because pride can take many forms within our lives. For instance, it manifests openly when we are quick to boast of our own works, argue our own ways, and refuse to listen to others.

In other ways, pride can remain unseen and unaddressed. It can be the root cause of our depression and frustrations toward ourselves. We can become depressed and frustrated in our thoughts, wondering why we keep failing, questioning why we can never cease our sinfulness, debating how we can save other people, and asking why we cannot change the minds of others. Without God, these thoughts can soon lead us into a pit of despair and destruction.

This leads us to ask, why did Paul boast of his weaknesses in 2 Corinthians 12:5-6? He wrote, "On behalf of such a one I will boast, but on my own behalf I will not boast, except in my weaknesses. For if I would desire to boast, I will not be foolish; for I will speak the truth. But I refrain, so that no man may think more of me than that which he sees in me, or hears from me."

He explained he would gladly boast of his fellow brethren but would only boast of his own weaknesses. But why? It is because Paul realized the strength of his pride and how easy it was to become overly "exalted" or "conceited" (2 Corinthians 12:7). However, instead of allowing his pride to overwhelm him, he chose to implement a practice to prevent his pride from consuming him. He used this practice to turn his mind from himself back onto God. Then why do we rarely boast of our weaknesses?

Do we not understand that our pride is the main culprit binding us to destruction? When puffing ourselves up, sharing our accomplishments while hiding our struggles, we replace God's strength for our own. Likewise, pride is often the root cause of our depression. When attempting to fight our lack of power by ourselves, thinking we can become stronger through our own means, we instead remove our source of strength.

In both cases, when thinking of ourselves as the source of strength, we bind ourselves to Satan. Our pride strips us of God, our true strength, and replaces Him with nothing more than a mirage. Because it is not our deeds that have strength by themselves, but God's power through our deeds that brings genuine success.

Then, why do we not implement the practices shown in Scripture meant to humble rather than enlarge our pridefulness? Why can we not humiliate ourselves? Do we fear what people would think if we were to reveal our shame?

Do we fear the mockery and jeering of the crowds more than our Lord? Do we fear the exposure of our failures while understanding that all fall short of the glory of God? Is it because we know they could see us as insignificant failures, perhaps thinking, "Why would God use someone like him?" Yet it would be these exact thoughts that would give glory back to God.

For at that moment, everyone would be reminded of the power of our King. They would see that God can use anyone, even the least. They would recognize that God's grace and mercy are for those who understand their shortcomings. For when we are weak, then we are strong (2 Corinthians 12:10).

Then let us no longer seek after our own strength if it is easy to be consumed by our pride, thinking of ourselves as being the reason for change. Rather, let us instill wise practices to fight against these pride-filled temptations by making it a constant habit to lower ourselves in front of others. Let us boast of our weaknesses and our failures.

For it is not the strength and power of men or women that we should seek. Even those in Scripture are but mere sinful beings like you and me who can hurt other people out of the desire for selfish gain. Consider the example of King David, who had his loyal man murdered out of his lust-filled desires for Bathsheba (2 Samuel 11-12). Or the apostle Paul, who murdered Christians out of his selfish pride and presumptions of greater understanding (Acts 8:1-3). They, too, were hard-headed, weakened by selfish beliefs.

Then why place weak men and women on pedestals when it is not they who have power? Rather, let us never forget that it is God's power through people that gives them their strength. It is their very shortcomings and failures shown within Scripture that give the ultimate glory to God. Therefore, we should never desire to replace God or elevate anyone above Him.

For it should be God that receives the glory over us. God is the One who turns us into shining examples, demonstrating that He can transform the weakest of us into the strongest. He is the power behind making even the least significant of actions into the most meaningful.

If we truly knew just how much grace and mercy was needed to redeem us, would we still be such a proud people? Would our desire continue to be for our own selfish gain? Would we continue thieving from the One who has already given, stealing His glory? Have we forgotten just how much was required for our redemption?

Do you ever wonder, "What is it that others see in me?" Is it my power, my strength, my desire, or is it my God, my Savior, my King? It shouldn't matter how little people think of us because our goal is not to please others but God alone (Galatians 1:10). We are and continue to be only weak people. We struggle with our sinful desires. Through the hardness of our hearts, we are but mere liars, murderers, thieves, and adulterers, a proud people.

For the desire to change our old ways should not be rooted in the belief of perfection through fleshly works. Rather, it is only out of God's love and mercy that we can even be guided toward His will. Therefore, let us not be proud of our strengths but of our weaknesses, refraining from becoming hypocrites. For it was not our power that changed us. We did not redeem ourselves. It was only through His love that we were given life. Our God is the one who saved us! Our God is the one who changed us!

7

Prayer and Meditation

Our sinful presumptions and heart mentalities can have much greater effects than we may first recognize. They can even end up clouding our most fundamental understandings of Scripture.

Many of us who have grown up within the church can presume that the base practices taught to us are automatically wise. We often believe that our elders and leaders can do no wrong. We regurgitate their man-made rules and laws to others and even use their exact reasonings as our own. We do this because it is easier for us to follow the masses instead of reading and studying the Scriptures for ourselves.

Currently, some of us may even remain in disbelief, shaking our heads in disagreement. For we cannot fathom that our core understanding of Scripture is false. We say that our foundational understanding of Scripture is strong.

But is it? Do we even know the importance of reading the Bible and praying in our own lives? If so, then why do we promote the practice of telling other believers that they should pray or read the Bible for an allotted amount of time per day?

What does the Bible say about this? Well, in Joshua 1:8, the Lord tells Joshua to meditate upon the book of the law day and night. And in 1 Thessalonians 5:17, the apostle Paul says to "pray without ceasing." Specifically, the Greek word used for "without ceasing" is "adialeiptōs," meaning uninterruptedly or permanently. In both places, we are not told to read the Bible or pray for a specific amount of time, but to continuously and uninterruptedly pray and meditate upon the Scriptures. Why is this important?

First, to meditate on something means one already knows what that something is. Therefore, to meditate on Scripture assumes one already knows the content of Scripture. Second, both passages show that this process is without end. And third, both are commands, which implies that should one not do this, they would be in sin.

In other words, when we cease our communication with God at any moment, even in that brief second of time, we are in sin! This is because when ignoring the Lord, we are, in essence, desiring to do our way over His.

Then, why do we ask others to pray for ten minutes, half an hour, or an hour when the counterargument implies that we desire them to be in sin for the remaining period? One may argue that the practice is for new believers to slowly strengthen their desire to pray and meditate on Scripture.

However, is that same argument not also valid when attempting to combat other sinful acts? Then why do we not use the same reasonings when dealing with other sinful practices? Should we only commit murder ten minutes a day? Do we debate whether the practice of spending only half an hour a day in soberness is a good suggestion? Should we recommend taking an hour's break from committing adultery? May we be reminded that our desire is for perfection itself, not just self-betterment.

By making it more palatable to a broader audience, we can end up diluting Scripture. By pleading with others for just five minutes of daily prayer with the Lord, we risk making light of sin. We can transform the Christian walk from being a forever lifestyle into a five-minute workout routine, so to speak. Of course, as stated previously, we are free to recommend people to pray or read their Bibles an hour a day in a manner of speaking, and surely there have been times when God has used this practice to help someone.

However, in teaching this practice solely without the context of Scripture, have we not undermined Scripture? Because in Matthew 5:19, we are told by Jesus to never lessen the severity of the law. "Whoever, therefore, shall break one of these least commandments, and teach others to do so, shall be called least in the Kingdom of Heaven; but whoever shall do and teach them shall be called great in the Kingdom of Heaven."

Then, does our man-made rule of praying or reading the Scripture an hour a day lessen or enhance the law of unceasing prayer and meditation when taught without the correct context? Because we can only lessen the law if replacing a greater law with a lesser law. Therefore, we must ask ourselves if we are teaching this practice to replace the law or to enhance the law. Are we teaching this man-made law to feel better about our own shortcomings? Are we placing stumbling blocks before other Christians to believe falsely, that they only need to speak with the Lord at certain times rather than unceasingly?

Because the question has never been about whether we *can* but whether we *should*. With that in mind, I believe that the enforcement of reading or praying a set amount of time has been far more detrimental than helpful. For it has a much higher likelihood to be used out of context, lessening rather than emphasizing the importance of prayer and God's Word by implying that God needs us rather than we need Him.

It is likely to be used in place of Scripture rather than to enhance Scripture, implying that we should pat ourselves on the back when giving but a moment of our time to the Lord. When, to follow Him is not a matter of taking a few minutes or hours out of our day, but a constant unending battleground against our sinful nature and Satan himself.

A battle that requires unceasing meditation and prayer. A battle where every moment matters. A battle that would be fruitless if it were not for our Lord and Savior.

Let us not forget that the meditation of Scripture and prayer are our main lines of defense against the evil one. It is the Holy Spirit, God Himself, who is our current guide in place of the old laws (John 16:13). Yet, how can we let Him guide our path if we refuse to speak to Him, and how can we differentiate His voice apart from the deceiver's if we do not meditate on His Word in every moment? Therefore, we must be unrelenting in our prayer and Scripture meditation, never having a moment apart from Christ.

There should never remain a moment within our lives in which we are left alone without the voice of the Lord and His Word guiding our every decision and thought. However, the question remains. If we do not recommend setting limits on the practices of Scripture reading and prayer, what could we recommend to help stimulate the desire for constant meditation and prayer?

Because it is easier to point the finger without alternatives. Therefore, may we look at another option, a suggestion from Scripture, the practice of godly speech? For this practice derived from James 3:1-10 has greatly helped in my own walk with Christ.

8

Focusing on Our Speech

¹ Let not many of you be teachers, my brothers, knowing that we will receive heavier judgment. ² For in many things we all stumble. If anyone doesn't stumble in word, the same is a perfect man, able to bridle the whole body also. ³ Indeed, we put bits into the horses' mouths so that they may obey us, and we guide their whole body. ⁴ Behold, the ships also, though they are so big and are driven by fierce winds, are yet guided by a very small rudder, wherever the pilot desires. ⁵ So the tongue is also a little member, and boasts great things. See how a small fire can spread to a large forest! ⁶ And the tongue is a fire. The world of iniquity among our members is the tongue, which defiles the whole body, and sets on fire the course of na-

ture, and is set on fire by Gehenna. ⁷ For every kind of animal, bird, creeping thing, and thing in the sea, is tamed, and has been tamed by mankind. ⁸ But nobody can tame the tongue. It is a restless evil, full of deadly poison. ⁹ With it we bless our God and Father, and with it we curse men, who are made in the image of God. ¹⁰ Out of the same mouth comes forth blessing and cursing. My brothers, these things ought not to be so.

In this passage, James, the half-brother of Jesus, presents the topic of godly speech by demonstrating the tongue's power over the body. He makes this clear by using illustrations like a bit controlling a horse or a rudder controlling a ship. And, by taking it a step further in verse 2, he explains that if we did not stumble in our words we would be "perfect."

However, other English Bible translations use the word "mature" instead of "perfect." This difference in translation comes from the varied interpretations of the Greek word "teleios." But why does it matter if there is a difference between English translations?

It is important because biblical scholars remain divided on the meaning of this verse. In this specific context, some believe that the original Greek word "teleios" means a full completion, hence the word "perfect." But others believe it describes a process, like a child growing into an adult, hence the word "mature." Therefore, James is either stating that watching our speech addresses all sins and can make one perfect if done flawlessly, or that watching one's speech can only help us grow in our walks with Christ.

However, there is one main reason "perfect" is the correct translation. This is because in verse 8, James explains it is impossible for one to control their tongue perfectly. So why does he bother elaborating that it is unattainable or unachievable if it is just a maturation process? Is James implying that we cannot grow as Christ-followers? Of course not. This makes no sense whatsoever because of the constant reminders found in Scripture that tell us otherwise (Ephesians 4:13-15). Therefore, James is stating that perfect speech leads to perfect control of one's body. But why is this so important?

This is important because it implies that perfect godly speech equals perfection itself. It indicates that the sole practice of watching our speech can deal with all sins. This is why James needed to emphasize that it is impossible to achieve perfect speech in verse 8. He had to clarify that we cannot be perfect in our current mortal bodies.

Surely, there are some who have quickly dismissed this claim, but it is important to note how the practice of solely watching our speech can address all sins within our lives. So, how can this practice address all sins?

Most commonly, people have problems with this claim because when thinking of the word "speech" they only think about "outward speech." They assume that speech only includes the physical aspect of talking, when in reality there is another type of speech. This other type would be best classified as "inner speech."

Inner speech is just as it sounds; it is our mental thoughts. Things like praying to the Lord, the meditations of Scripture, and how we address our sins from within are all included within the purview of inner speech. Therefore, focusing on the practice of godly speech can allow us to fully address everything—both outward actions and inward heart mentalities. Then, what difference does it make whether we focus on the practice of godly speech instead of other traditional methods of spiritual growth?

First, the practice of godly speech can help guide us to immediate action by preventing the delay between thinking of what we should do and actually doing it. For example, the thought "How can I speak in a manner that is honoring to you, Lord?" can already begin to please the Lord.

This question can immediately remove any delay between thinking and doing, for the thought itself is the application. However, many spiritual applications require a thought phase and an application point. For example, to practice reading one's Bible, one must first decide to set a time to physically do it, then wait until that time to do it. These delays in between are what Satan can use against us to tempt us into laziness or procrastination.

This is yet another reason why we are told to "meditate" on Scripture (Joshua 1:8) rather than just "read" Scripture. As "meditation" can be done immediately without having to physically "read" the Scriptures. Therefore, the practice of godly speech has an advantage over many other spiritual practices because of how quickly it can be implemented.

Second, as shown previously, the practice of godly speech can cover all areas of our spiritual walks with Christ by addressing both heart mentalities and the works that come from them. It can even cover the practice of meditating on Scripture and prayer with the Lord. Therefore, it is a rare practice that can help in every aspect of our walks with Christ. By learning to listen and speak with God, ourselves, and others, we can use godly speech as a tool to help guide any other practices rooted in Scripture.

Finally, focusing on our speech and how we talk can help us turn our attention to others. Because often when we think of the word "speech," we think of our physical speech toward others; we immediately think of talking with others when being told to "talk." Yet when we think about what we should do as Christ-followers, what are most commonly our first thoughts?

When asked, "What should we do as Christ-followers?" Many would certainly think, "I should focus on my personal relationship with God." Our initial thoughts are usually to focus on ourselves. They probably aren't going to think,

"I should spend more time with others to help focus my attention back to God."

But why does this matter? It matters because while there are times it is necessary to be alone with the Lord, we are shown time and again that God desires us to seek after others. Then, why do many believe we can grow in Christ by ignoring others if the second greatest commandment, shown in Mark 12:31, is to love others. Additionally, the Great Commission commands us to go and make disciples (Matthew 28:16-20).

Let us not forget that Jesus Himself explains the importance of loving others. He tells us we should seek reconciliation even before attempting to bring gifts before Him in Matthew 5:23-24: "If therefore you are offering your gift at the altar, and there remember that your brother has anything against you, leave your gift there before the altar, and go your way. First be reconciled to your brother, and then come and offer your gift."

Is it any wonder why some of us rarely hear God's voice? For if we have little urgency to speak and be reconciled with others, how can we say we are following Jesus? Then how can we stop ignoring others? We can stop ignoring others by learning how to speak with them in a God-centered way.

Therefore, by the pure implication of the word "speech," the practice of godly speech can help focus our attention on others instead of only ourselves. Then is not godly speech a wise practice that has its own unique merits outside of other spiritual practices? It can guide us away from the temptation of laziness by focusing us immediately on the Lord. It can cover all other spiritual practices and even help us focus on others rather than ourselves.

However, I am sure there are still many who would still shake their heads in disagreement with this practice, arguing about how James did not clearly state this practice, and I would not argue with them. Because we are indeed free from the law.

But why do we often try to dismiss any law that could enhance our walk with Christ, helping us to be unceasing in prayer and meditation? And why instead, are we so accepting of other man-made practices that reduce the laws of Scripture transforming unceasing prayer to only an hour of prayer?

Regardless, the Bible is clear that speech is an important part of our walk as Christ-followers. Then an obvious question remains: Do we even understand the most fundamental biblical teachings that pertain to speaking with one another, or does this remain but another false presumption?

9

Learning to Listen

We are told to be quick to hear and slow to talk in James 1:19: "So, then, my beloved brothers, let every man be swift to hear, slow to speak, and slow to anger."

But what does the word "hear" describe? The word "hear" in James 1:19 comes from the Greek word "akouó." It means to "give heed to" or "understand." In other words, we are called as Christians to be quick to understand.

Yet when communicating with others, are our first thoughts to attempt to understand what is being spoken before responding? Do we even understand the words that we are hearing?

Because it is mainly through our words that we communicate with others, but words can carry many meanings within a plethora of contexts. Sometimes we may even ignore, forget, or misuse a word's definition.

So how can we begin to understand others if we do not even bother to know what they are attempting to convey? We must consider what people are trying to tell us when they speak, what the meaning behind their words is, whether we are even talking about the same thing, and whether our word definitions are the same.

For example, the word "home" can describe many things. It could describe a physical place of residence like somewhere we currently live, a place we grew up in, or even a place where loved ones are. One definition could refer to the heart condition of "home" while another could refer to the actual physical manifestation of "home."

Therefore, why do we not ask questions to clarify which definition is being referred to? Dare we respond to others or our God without even first attempting to understand what is being said? Because sometimes our presumptions about word definitions can lead to critical misunderstandings if we misinterpret others' words.

One such case was with my understanding of the word "Christian." While growing up in the church, I was always told that we should never be romantically involved with nonbelievers. I was taught that we should only date other "Christians."

The reasoning behind this is found in 2 Corinthians 6:14. This is the verse that Paul used to explain how we should not be "unequally yoked," or bound, with nonbelievers. He wrote, "Don't be unequally yoked with unbelievers, for what fellowship have righteousness and iniquity? Or what fellowship has light with darkness?"

Yet what was Paul trying to say when speaking these words? For the longest time, I struggled with understanding his meaning. Because truthfully, I saw little difference between the people who claimed to be "Christian" and those outside the church. The sad reality was that I truly felt as if the lifestyles of those outside of the church were sometimes more in line with Scripture than those who called themselves "Christians."

It was later that I realized the meaning of the word "Christian." It is not just a title. It is not only a claim to be "Christian" but a reference to those who truly follow Christ. For Paul was not referring to a title, but a lifestyle. He explained we should not be bound to people who are unbelievers, for they do not share the same beliefs as those who are of God.

Therefore, we should be wary of attaching ourselves to those who live lives in contrast to or in defiance to our Lord. Because the word "Christian" does not equate to a mere title, but to one who truly believes and follows Christ. For while "Christian" should be synonymous with "Christ-follower," the unfortunate truth is that many times it is not.

It is for these reasons that my understanding of Scripture became compromised with the simple misunderstanding of the word "Christian." In turn, this small misunderstanding led me to be with people who I should not have been with. This mistake caused me to stumble greatly in my walk with Christ. Yet, correcting my understanding of the definition of "Christian" eventually helped lead me to find my wife: my best friend, my greatest supporter, my love.

Through this example, hopefully we now see the importance of words. So, what does it mean to "hear" as stated in James 1:19? Is the purpose of hearing to just understand the words of others? Is it to simply become great debaters? Do we only listen for the purpose of reinforcing our own presumptions and proving ourselves right? Of course not.

Then, what exactly are we attempting to understand when we are told to be "quick to hear"? Let us not forget what Jesus said in Matthew 6:24: "No one can serve two masters, for either he will hate the one and love the other; or else he will be devoted to one and despise the other. You can't serve both God and Mammon."

In other words, there are only two possible reasons behind every action because we can only serve one master or another. Therefore, we must evaluate which master we are serving. For we are either following Christ or following Satan, a fact that remains true even among the practices found in Scripture. Then what does this mean? This means that there are two separate meanings behind being "quick to hear."

The first definition is the practical application of listening. It defines the "how" part of hearing. How can we listen to and understand others? However, the second definition deals with the heart condition of hearing, the "why" part of listening. Why should we be quick to listen?

Should we not then ask ourselves if our practices of listening are being done in the correct heart mentality? Who are we listening to? Are we trying to hear our own inner arguments and Satan first, or are we trying to hear the voice of our Lord regardless of how we feel at the moment?

It is important to make this distinction, for the purpose of being "quick to hear" is to discern the voice of God. Therefore, we should always seek to hear God's voice, even through what others are saying. For His voice is what we are attempting to discern when listening to other's criticisms, arguments, and encouragements. Even when we are in the simplest of conversations, our gaze should be focused on our Lord.

This heart of listening can be seen in the example of King David in 2 Samuel 16:7-12. When King David was fleeing from his kingdom and his own son Absalom, a man named Shimei came out to mock and curse him:

> Shimei said when he cursed, "Be gone, be gone, you man of blood, and base fellow! Yahweh has returned on you all the blood of the house of Saul, in whose place you have reigned! Yahweh has delivered the kingdom into the hand of Absalom your son! Behold, you are caught by

your own mischief, because you are a man of blood!" (2 Samuel 16:7-8)

It was here, in this moment, that King David was pushed to the extreme. For even as he was losing his home, family, and everything he held most dear to him, Shimei came out to mock and badger him. Shimei shouted insult after insult at David, trying to taunt him.

What would we do if our best friend was being attacked in the same manner as King David? Would our response to this not have been to return insults, get payback, or even worse? Likewise, one of King David's men, Abishai, thought similarly. In 2 Samuel 16:9, Abishai told King David, "Why should this dead dog curse my lord the king? Please let me go over and take off his head."

Yet let us consider how King David responded to this request to kill Shimei. In 2 Samuel 16:11-12, David tells his men, "Leave him alone, and let him curse; for Yahweh has invited him. It may be that Yahweh will look on the wrong done to me, and that Yahweh will repay me good for the cursing of me today."

King David decided to listen to the Lord instead of responding in anger and rage. Despite what he may have felt, he first sought to hear the Lord's voice. Regardless of whether or not Shimei was speaking wrongfully, David used Shimei's hate-filled words meant to curse him as a tool to humble him. He attempted to discern God's will and be further strengthened by the Lord.

However, this does not mean that King David had no emotions when Shimei cursed him. For he remembered these curses even on his deathbed. They plagued his mind for so long that King David had Shimei put to death after his passing. In 1 Kings 2:8-9, he said:

> Behold, there is with you Shimei the son of Gera, the Benjamite, of Bahurim, who cursed me with a grievous curse in the day when I went to Mahanaim; but he came down to meet me at the Jordan, and I swore to him by Yahweh, saying, "I will not put you to death with the sword." Now therefore don't hold him guiltless, for you are a wise man; and you will know what you ought to do to him, and you shall bring his gray head down to Sheol with blood.

In other words, even though the hateful words of Shimei had most likely enraged King David, he still attempted to hear God's voice through them. Then, let us ask ourselves, for what reason are we listening to others? Are we listening out of our sinfulness or are we listening to hear the Lord?

For many times, we remain enraged by the words of those in authority over us. But God did not place the family structure (Ephesians 5:22-6:4), elders (1 Peter 5:5), and governing authorities (Romans 13:1) over us for no reason. Then, why do we tend to see these authority figures as adversaries to defeat rather than as guards who can protect us from the wants and self-desires of our sinful hearts?

These same people God placed over us may just be the "thorns" given in our lives to keep our egos in check, as Paul shares in 2 Corinthians 12:7, "By reason of the exceeding greatness of the revelations, that I should not be exalted excessively, there was given to me a thorn in the flesh, a messenger of Satan to torment me, that I should not be exalted excessively."

What then are your minds currently dwelling on while going through this written work? Have you been trying to deconstruct every sentence as you read? Has your anger overtaken you, or have you been trying to listen to the Lord reaching out to you? How can these words, erroneous or not, be used to help you in your own walk with Christ?

10

Words of "Good" Intention

Even our responses toward others can be rooted in sinful desire rather than desire for the Lord. For as shown earlier, all actions and practices can be done in righteousness or in sinfulness. Then how can our speech with others be contaminated by Satan? By thinking that we have "good" intentions, Satan can sometimes use these presumptions to do far more damage than we realize.

In 1 Peter 3:15, we are told to always be ready to make a defense for why we believe in Jesus: "But sanctify the Lord God in your hearts; and always be ready to give an answer to everyone who asks you a reason concerning the hope that is in you, with humility and fear."

This is why we should always be mentally prepared to answer others' questions about what we believe. Yet, sometimes in thinking we are defending our views for the right reasons, we are instead defending them out of sinful desire. We can end up overlooking the Lord while trying to become the "winner" and forget that the argument itself has no power to win over the other person.

Many times, I often have to remind myself of this very pitfall. Because it can feel good to silence the opposing view. It can be exciting to have the crowds be in awe of eloquent answers rooted in undeniable logic. But should this be our only motivation for speaking up?

Once, I had gotten into a debate with someone who wished to know why I believed in God, for he believed it was utter foolishness to believe in a God. I went on to argue with him, with one answer after another. This debate soon attracted many onlookers, for they, too, were interested in the responses given.

With each man's pride at stake now, I refused to lose. I had truth on my side and, therefore, I would use all at my disposal to destroy any argument, taking from my opposer any shred of dignity he may have had left. As the debate raged further, my opponent became infuriated, for his arguments had lost all ground. As the crowds became more and more enamored, the Lord asked me, "Is this the reason you speak?"

I was reminded in that moment of why we should speak to begin with and that having great arguments should not be the sole reason we do anything. For we are not only called to make a defense of our faith but also to do it with love.

As 1 Corinthians 16:14 says, "Let all that you do be done in love."

I had forgotten that we are to always speak truth in love. Because without love, without God, even the best defenses have no power to change. Then why was I defending my viewpoints? Was I doing it because I loved my opponent and wanted him to see that God loved him? No, I was now only arguing out of a sense of self-gratification and pride.

My heart mentality was in the wrong, and I quickly attempted to resolve this mistake. It was here that I ordered the onlookers to disperse and leave, for this conversation would no longer be a show. It was here that I spoke one-on-one with my fellow debater. It was here that I finally saw him as a fellow man whom God also loved instead of an opponent to face.

I wanted him to know that the purpose of my defense was not supposed to be rooted in a desire to be a better debater. I wanted him to know that it was because God loved him, and therefore I loved him. This is the moment that God used the conversation for His good. Instead of further anger and resentment, God reached out and opened his eyes in this moment, tearing down the walls of anger and frustration that once seemed impenetrable.

Yet often in the middle of our arguments, we can be swept up in the moment. We can forget the first part of 1 Peter 3:15. We can forget to "sanctify the Lord God" in our hearts before making our statements. It is here that we must ask ourselves again, is there any purpose in even the best defenses if spoken from the wrong heart mentality?

We live in a world today where many do not even claim to believe in a god. They believe everything started from nothing, that nothing turned into something, that anything can become anything else, and that we live in a random universe.

Yet these people who believe that anything can happen are the same people who call Christians insane for believing that God created everything. They believe that anything can happen except the existence of a god or supreme ruler. The only thing they refuse to believe is that there may be another with power over them. With this understanding, will we continue deluding ourselves into believing that better logical reasonings alone will change their minds? Is that not insanity?

We wish to change their hearts through reasonings and deductions. Yet our actions are only given strength when done with the right heart mentality. Our strength comes from God alone.

Must we again be reminded of whom we serve? Even the apostle Paul reminds us of this matter in Romans 6:16: "Don't you know that to whom you present yourselves as servants to obedience, his servants you are whom you obey; whether of sin to death, or of obedience to righteousness?"

In other words, the apostle Paul again reminds us plainly that we can be either servants to our sins in death or to the Lord our God. Therefore, even "good" intentions mean nothing without the Lord. If anything, our "good" intentions often remain only as another deceit from the devil to forget about God, for anything done without the Lord is for the devil. For without the Lord, our arguments, regardless of how accurate they may be, are only rooted in sin and death.

For even if we have a stronger understanding of Scripture or a better logical argument, it does not make it okay to share our knowledge with the wrong heart mentality. In 1 Corinthians 13:1, we are shown that without having the right heart mentality, we lose all power to change others, becoming only an annoying alarm and nuisance for others: "If I speak with the languages of men and of angels, but don't have love, I have become sounding brass, or a clanging cymbal."

As shown previously, there are times when the Lord has called others to do something. Some Christians may be called to go to dangerous locations to spread the gospel. Others could be called to be bold and rely on the Lord for their health.

Yet often there are times when we place stumbling blocks in front of loved ones who choose to follow the Lord and go against what we deem as safe and popular. We can become a hindrance to our fellow brothers and sisters in Christ by replacing the Lord's voice with our own.

One example of this is found in Matthew 16:21-23. In verse 21, Jesus began to share with His disciples that He was being called to go away. He explained how He would suffer greatly and eventually be crucified: "From that time, Jesus began to show his disciples that he must go to Jerusalem and suffer many things from the elders, chief priests, and scribes, and be killed, and the third day be raised up."

It is here that many Christ-followers, if put in a similar situation as the disciples, would have spoken up. If our loved ones told us they were called by God to be martyrs for the gospel, we would probably tell them that they should not go. For who would wish to lose family members and loved ones, especially if we knew we could prevent it? Likewise, Peter, a disciple of Jesus, thought this way in verse 22: "Peter took him aside, and began to rebuke him, saying, 'Far be it from you, Lord! This will never be done to you.'"

But do you know what Jesus's response to this statement was? Instead of remaining silent or even responding "nicely," He rebuked Peter in verse 23, saying, "Get behind me, Satan! You are a stumbling block to me, for you are not setting your mind on the things of God, but on the things of men."

Likewise, many times we, too, become stumbling blocks to our fellow Christians, speaking up in similar situations when we should instead remain silent. We forget Exodus

20:7, which says we should not use God's name in vain: "You shall not take the name of Yahweh your God in vain, for Yahweh will not hold him guiltless who takes his name in vain."

For using the Lord's name in vain is not merely using a word inappropriately; it is a heart mentality as well. Then, are we not using God's name in vain when we dare to speak in the Lord's place, replacing His name with our own? We often speak up without first consulting our God in prayer and end up telling others what to do from our own sinful mentalities.

We make excuses for our behaviors, saying they are out of love or compassion. When in reality we are only being used by Satan, placing stumbling blocks before others who are attempting to follow Jesus. We can unintentionally tell others to follow worldly desires instead of God's desires.

It is important to remember that we should always be "quick to hear" if God is speaking through our words. However, if we do not feel as if God wants us to speak, then why do we speak at all? Because the honest truth is that if we continue to speak out of turn, we deserve any and every rebuke from the Lord. For if we dare to replace God's words with our own, placing stumbling blocks before others, we have become slaves to Satan.

However, while the dangers of speaking are surely there, the dangers of silence are equally threatening. For silence does not equal listening because it is just as easy to ignore others while speaking over them as it is to ignore them by daydreaming and remaining silent. Therefore, if we refuse to speak up in fear of unpopularity, worldly consequences, or laziness, we also remain in sin.

Then why do we remain silent, continuing to avert our eyes when others place stumbling blocks against us? For if we allow our fellow Christians to remain ignorant of their ways, are we not also responsible? Did we forget Ephesians 5:11, which says that we are to expose and reprove sin? "Have no fellowship with the unfruitful works of darkness, but rather even reprove them."

If not, then let us no longer remain silent when God calls us to speak, and let us no longer speak without God telling us to. Let us be bold in calling out the sins of other Christians when they attempt to teach us to disobey our Lord, and let us be humble enough to not always have the last word.

For our goal is not to speak out more frequently or less frequently. Our goal is to realize that without the right heart mentalities, our actions, regardless of how "nice" or "good" they are, have no power. For our power comes from God, and our acts can only represent our Lord or Satan. There is no in-between.

Is it then any wonder why many of our churches have become filled with only barren land when our speech lacks any sort of discernment, exhortation, or love? For we tend to cower in fear when we realize that speaking truth may make us unpopular, yet we remain bold when we want to get the final word for our own sake. Therefore, we must remain vigilant before the Lord, for the dangers of both speaking and remaining silent are always present.

Then, should our quick listening and slow speech with others start from our external voice? Of course not. It is from within that we derive our outward speech. Then how can we address our internal voice?

11

Wholistic Worldview

God willing, we have now seen how our external speech is meaningless without the correct heart mentality behind it. For our speech is but the outpouring of what hides in our hearts, as explained by Jesus in Matthew 15:18, "But the things which proceed out of the mouth come out of the heart, and they defile the man."

However, as discussed earlier, speech does not just include how we speak externally but internally as well. Therefore, even our prayers with God and the meditations of Scripture can be done improperly. Because even "good" spiritual practices found in Scripture are meaningless without the Lord, as clearly seen in the modern age.

We have seen many who know the Scriptures and pray only to mock and belittle our Lord. They read the Scriptures to misquote and taunt. They pray out loud, mocking the Lord for not striking them down at that very moment. Likewise, can we not also treat Scripture and prayer similarly? Are there not also times we can treat God like a wishing well or twist Scripture to promote our own agendas? For there is no doubt the reason many do not believe in the power of prayer is because of their improper speech with the Lord.

Then, if we know that our sinful hearts can cloud and distort even the best of practices, we must cleanse these foggy lenses to gain discernment in our walks with Christ. But how do we gain the wisdom in Christ to know what we should or should not do if our sinful hearts can deceive us on such fundamental levels?

It is for this reason that Jesus teaches us how to pray in Matthew 6:9-10, "Pray like this: 'Our Father in heaven, may your name be kept holy. Let your Kingdom come. Let your will be done, as in heaven, so on earth.'"

Jesus shows us through His example that the first thing we should do when speaking to the Lord is to seek after God's will. We must seek after our Lord in all earnestness and sincerity, chasing after His desire over all else. For there is no true power in anything we do without the Lord's strength behind our actions.

Therefore, let us first start by praying for God's will to be done over our will and to be humbled always. Because it is only after being humbled before the Lord that we can discern God's voice from Satan's. But how can we know our God's desire? We can start to know our God's desire by gaining a wholistic view of Scripture rather than picking and choosing the parts that best suit us.

Because, as sinful beings, we can fail to recognize the dangers of categorizing things within our minds. Many times, we can end up focusing on one topic while disregarding another, since it is usually simpler to focus on one task at hand rather than keep everything in mind. However, this preference has caused many problems in our biblical worldviews.

We like to separate things from each other, like the Old Testament from the New Testament. But it was Jesus who said that He came to fulfill the laws of old rather than destroy them. In Matthew 5:17, He said, "Don't think that I came to destroy the law or the prophets. I didn't come to destroy, but to fulfill." Therefore, the New Testament complements the Old Testament rather than replaces it.

In other words, the Bible should not be interpreted as separate parts, from one passage to another, but as a whole. This is similar to how our body is not a mere brain—our muscles, bones, limbs, and organs all serve their respective parts in helping us function properly. It is for this reason that we should think through the lens of "both/together" instead of "this/that."

For every part of the Bible is needed in our Christian walk, as shown in 2 Timothy 3:16-17, "Every Scripture is God-breathed and profitable for teaching, for reproof, for correction, and for instruction in righteousness, that the man of God may be complete, thoroughly equipped for every good work."

Then, if we should view the Bible as a whole rather than as individual pieces, why do we have such trouble interpreting Scripture through the lens of the heart rather than the law? Because if we are free from the law, then every law, including even those in the New Testament, must be interpreted as God attempting to challenge our hearts rather than just following more rules blindly.

Even the Lord's prayer is but another example of how we can mistake the heart for the law. Then, what is the rest of Jesus's prayer in Matthew 6:9-10? What else should we do after seeking the Lord's will? It is here that we find one of the most vital pieces of our speech with the Lord. Finishing in verses 11-13, Jesus stated, "Give us today our daily bread. Forgive us our debts, as we also forgive our debtors. Bring us not into temptation, but deliver us from the evil one. For yours is the Kingdom, the power, and the glory forever. Amen."

But what is the purpose of asking for our "daily bread," to be forgiven as we "forgive our debtors," to not be brought into "temptation," and to "deliver us from the evil one"? Does Jesus say these things to give us another law? Are we to repeat word for word new statements to become enslaved by mere words? Rather, is not the purpose to identify whether our hearts are truly humbled before the Lord?

Because to first ask for our "daily bread" is to be reminded of who gives us our basic needs. It means that we should remember to be grateful for everything and that it is only through God that we receive anything. For even our daily necessities come from God, as He is the ultimate Creator and supplier.

Second, to state that we desire forgiveness as we "forgive our debtors" is to remember God's desire for others and choose it over our own. As we remember from Matthew 5:23-24, God tells us He finds it more important for us to seek reconciliation with others than even to present gifts before Him.

Third, to not be brought into "temptation" is to realize the dangers of our hearts; understanding that we can be easily swayed into the wrong heart mentality. For as we have seen so far, even the most mundane things can be a tool for the devil to use against us.

Finally, to ask God to "deliver us from the evil one" is to recognize that only God has the power to help us in our fight against our sinful natures and the devil. For we are powerless without Him by our side.

Therefore, the purpose of asking for our "daily bread," to be forgiven as we "forgive our debtors," to not be brought into "temptation," and to "deliver us from the evil one" is to determine if we are truly humbled before the Lord. They are tools Jesus uses to exemplify a humble heart in His example of prayer. In other words, they are four identification markers to see if our hearts truly desire God's will over our own.

Because how can we believe we are truly humble before the Lord if we cannot recognize that He is the ultimate provider, cannot see that He is the only One that has power over sin, and continue in our bitterness against others? As it is impossible to be humbled before the Lord if we refuse to do what He has already shown in Scripture.

Since, the idea of a perfect God redeeming us from our sin is incomparable to sinful people forgiving the mistakes of others. It is like being given a million dollars by a stranger, only to remember that someone else owed you a single dollar and sue them over it (Matthew 18:21-34). How can we believe that we have any sort of appreciation for what we have been given if we continue to dwell upon the single dollar that we are owed?

Likewise, it is impossible to understand the gravity of our sin if we cannot forgive others for their sins against us. Whether we have never understood or only need reminding, I do not know. But it is for these reasons that Jesus gives us a dire warning if we choose not to forgive others: "But if you don't forgive men their trespasses, neither will your Father forgive your trespasses" (Matthew 6:15).

And if humility before the Lord is truly what we seek, then why should we separate the time spent between our Lord and everything else? Because being humbled and desiring

His will over our own is the reason we are to be unceasing in our prayers before Him.

Therefore, our time being humbled before God should not differ from our time outside of church service, with others, or even by ourselves. Praying humbly before our Lord is something that must remain constant throughout every thought in every moment. For our hearts are constantly at war with the evil one, and every moment that we remain apart from Him is the same as us being against Him.

In other words, we need Him in everything, not just in times of dire need or crucial moments. Then why do we not consult God about what groceries we should purchase, who we should spend our time with, or even how to rest? Why are we not constantly asking, "Are these actions wise to do according to Scripture?" For even the smallest of our decisions should not be made without guidance from God.

And if we understand the importance of viewing prayer in its entirety rather than partially, why do we view the rest of Scripture as separate? Is not the understanding of Scripture required to hear His voice more clearly? Because it is important to know how to listen to God after speaking with Him.

Therefore, it is not only our prayer and speech toward God that must be seen as a whole; we must learn how to listen and hear God as well. The meditation of Scripture itself must be interpreted as a whole, or else it, too, can be used as a weapon by Satan (Matthew 4:6). It can be turned into a tool only used for seeking approval of our own ways over the Lord's.

Since we all have tendencies that Satan can use to deceive us. For example, some of us may overly focus on the positive aspects of Scripture, failing to address sin due to its "negativity." And others of us could dwell too long in negative thoughts, forgetting the good news of the gospel, forgetting that God continues to love and desire us despite our shortcomings.

But have we ever wondered why we are told to always be joyful? In 1 Thessalonians 5:16, God instructs us, "Rejoice always." Yet the same Bible also tells us to "abhor," or hate, sin in Romans 12:9, "Let love be without hypocrisy. Abhor that which is evil. Cling to that which is good."

It is because joy and hate are not in contradiction with one another when implemented correctly. Rather, they are both different sides of the same coin, so to speak, because the same reasons we are to always rejoice are why we are also to be angry with our sinfulness. How can we be healed of something if we do not admit to being sick? For we must recognize the problem of sin if we are to understand our sickness, and it is only through understanding our sickness that we can recognize why we should be joyful.

Because we were healed from no mere disease. Our sickness was so vile that it corrupted everything it touched. Regardless of man, woman, or child, all were infected. But it was only through the overabundant grace and mercy of the ultimate healer, God in flesh, that our sinful nature, this abhorrent disease, could even be redeemed (2 Corinthians 5:21).

Then if joy and hate should be viewed together rather than separate, why is it so difficult to desire justice while also having compassion for those who have wronged others (Zechariah 7:9-10)? Why is it that we instead stoop down to the level of those who do not claim to be of God? Because in Ephesians 5:4, we are told not to speak or jest in immoral foolishness: "nor filthiness, nor foolish talking, nor jesting, which are not appropriate; but rather giving of thanks."

Yet, we are often caught mocking those outside the church. We laugh and joke at the expense of those who do not claim to be of God. Instead of turning the other cheek, we repay evil with evil. Does it benefit us to revert back to our old ways? If we wish to mock, then why not mock ourselves for returning to our old ways? For at least then we would be reminded of our sinfulness.

But besides Scripture needing to be viewed as a whole, should not everything be viewed as a whole rather than separate? Because it is not only Scripture that helps determine God's will for us, for as shown in Romans 1:20, the world reflects God and also helps us perceive Him: "For the invisible things of him since the creation of the world are clearly seen, being perceived through the things that are made, even his everlasting power and divinity; that they may be without excuse."

Therefore, if this world can reflect God and His will for us, then a wholistic view of Scripture includes having an accurate biblical worldview. For, a wholistic view of Scripture includes how we view the world. This means we can also use statistics and facts as another way to help us discern God's voice and desires. As long as we remain vigilant in seeking after our Lord, everything can help us better understand Him. For God can speak to us through all means, whether it be through dreams, the world, or others.

Yet this only remains good if we view it through the lens of God and His Word because it is easy to become ensnared by Satan and his false ideologies. It is vital to stay humbled before God while having a wholistic view of Scripture, for only God can give us correct discernment, and it is mainly through Scripture that God helps us understand His will.

Then how can we gain greater clarity to discern our Lord's voice from Satan's? We can do this by utilizing the other tools in Scripture that teach us how to deal with our sin-filled heart mentalities.

12

Gaining Discernment

In 1 Corinthians 5:12, Paul tells the congregation at Corinth to deal with the sinful behaviors running rampant within their church: "For what have I to do with also judging those who are outside? Don't you judge those who are within?"

Therefore, we are called to discern between the rights and wrongs in the body of Christ. But we are called to first discern our own issues and problems, as Jesus explained in Matthew 7:3-5:

> Why do you see the speck that is in your brother's eye, but don't consider the beam that is in your own eye? Or how will you tell your brother, "Let me remove the speck from your eye;" and behold, the beam is in your own eye? You hypocrite! First remove the beam out of your own

eye, and then you can see clearly to remove the speck out of your brother's eye.

Within this passage, Jesus told His listeners to deal with their own sins first before trying to find the faults in others. Likewise, we are to first address our own addictions before pointing the finger at the sins of others. Yet, how can we address our sinfulness?

We can start by implementing the biblical practice of testing ourselves. This is a practice that is mentioned throughout Scripture, including when Paul addressed it in 2 Corinthians 13:5-6, "Test your own selves, whether you are in the faith. Test your own selves. Or don't you know as to your own selves, that Jesus Christ is in you?—unless indeed you are disqualified. But I hope that you will know that we aren't disqualified."

Paul explained the purpose of "testing ourselves" in the faith. He argued that we should examine ourselves *not* for the purpose of boasting but to see whether God is truly first in our lives. In other words, this is a practice designed to help us identify addictions and to repent of our sinful ways.

But what does it mean to "test ourselves"? For as stated previously, all practices can be done in sin or righteousness. Therefore, the practice of testing ourselves must first be an action that attempts to discern whether God remains first in our lives. Second, it should not be a test that tries to tempt us or others into sinning. However, other than needing to fit within these parameters, these tests can be as unique as you and me.

In other words, a self-test must be designed to challenge our own sinfulness without tempting us to sin in the process. By bringing to light our own weaknesses and shortcomings, these self-tests can help us in our daily battles against sin. Yet now that we know how to test ourselves, the larger question remains: Are we willing to test ourselves to find our own shortcomings, or do we wish to be told by God that our faith in Christ was not genuine in our final moments before the judgment seat?

Because many times, when challenged in our walks of faith, we become defensive. We make excuses for why we do not need to be challenged. We tell ourselves that we do not need any self-tests because we already know what would happen. We create idealistic scenarios in our minds, thinking that we would definitely give up anything for God as long as He told us to. However, these imaginary scenarios are only theories when untested in reality.

For the Lord has already told us through His Word that He, too, desires to expose our shortcomings. As Jeremiah 17:10 says, "I, Yahweh, search the mind, I try the heart, even to give every man according to his ways, according to the fruit of his doings."

Then why are we so quick to dismiss the challenges in Scripture as being unapplicable to our own lives? For example, the story of the rich young man in Matthew 19:16-22 again comes to mind.

In verse 21, we clearly see how Jesus asked the rich man to sell all his possessions. Jesus said, "If you want to be perfect, go, sell what you have, and give to the poor, and you will have treasure in heaven; and come, follow me."

Yet, when hearing this statement, many of us are quick to argue that this same challenge Jesus gave to the rich man does not pertain to us. But why not? Are we not free to do anything as long as we do it for the Lord? Are we not called to test ourselves to see whether we would choose God above all, including all our material goods?

If the reason for testing ourselves is to see whether we actually desire God to be first in our lives, then why can we not also apply this challenge from Jesus as a test against our own addictions to material gain? Is it more important for us to keep all our material goods or to know if God is truly Lord of our lives? If not, then why do we not ask ourselves if we, too, are willing to give away all our possessions in order to follow Jesus?

By justifying our own excuses, we can be quick to explain how the harsh challenges in Scripture do not apply to us. We argue that such an action should not be done in practice. We say that it is not by works but by faith alone that we have been saved. We argue that God has never asked us specifically to do the same task and, therefore, we deny any need to mimic such a sacrificial test.

Yet, while many of these arguments may have some merit, let us be reminded that our sinful nature runs deep. It runs so deep that it can even deceive our thoughts (Jeremiah 17:9). The instruction that Paul gave to test ourselves was never about a performance of specific deeds for salvation, rather it was a wise practice rooted in faith. These self-tests are designed to expose the hidden truths of our own belief or disbelief.

Therefore, are not the challenges shown in Scripture applicable to our own lives? Did we forget it is not about what we *can* do, but what we *should* do? So why then do we quickly disregard the test of physically giving away all our possessions if we wish to know whether we would truly choose our Lord above all else?

Is it not merely because we do not wish to? Is it not but our sinful nature that attempts to excuse away any harsh test for our own lives? Because if we were honest, we would agree that it is of upmost importance to test ourselves—in even the most extreme ways—to see if God is truly worth more than everything.

However, for argument's sake, let us just assume that this specific test would not be wise to do in practice due to other applicable biblical reasonings or circumstances. For, as stated before, self-tests should not be done if their purpose is to tempt us or others into sin. Then why not have another test in its place?

Because thankfully, just as there are limitless excuses why we should not give away all our physical possessions, there are also endless possibilities for how we can still test ourselves. Therefore, why not try living momentarily without our things for a week, a month, a year? Why not give away more than ten percent, fifty percent, or eighty percent?

As we can see, self-tests are not limited to only specific scenarios. They are as flexible as we need them to be in order to challenge our faith in Christ and can be applied to everything. A self-test against modern comforts could lead us to live without electricity or running water for six months. To test ourselves on who we desire most could entail being single for a year. Testing to know whether we would be missionaries could challenge us to become actual missionaries for two years. The possibilities are endless.

Then why can we be so quick to make excuses that lead us toward inaction rather than action? It is, of course, easier to point at those dealing with addictions that are easily seen and say they are the ones who need to be tested. But, what about our own addictions, whether it be addiction to our ideas, leisurely activities, comfort zones, or finances? Because an addiction is any sin we refuse to address, even if we believe it to be of little importance. As we become enslaved to Satan when our minds are not dwelling upon the Lord (Romans 6:16).

And the honest truth is that many of us would rather live in continuous comfort than actually know if God is first in our lives. We wish to remain ignorant of our addictions to material gain and our struggles of self-desire. Yet how can we boast of our weaknesses and His strength while refusing to acknowledge and confess our own problems?

Are we afraid of failure, knowing God has already paid the ultimate price? Have we been in denial the entire time? Are we afraid others might see our weaknesses? Would we rather find out the truth behind our hearts only in our final moments? If not, then we should test against the things we desire.

In my experience, this topic has always received the greatest pushback because to confront our addictions we must first admit to them. This is why I also struggled to see my own shortcomings. I wanted to live in my excuses and idealisms so that my life could be as pleasurable as possible.

Yet, as I stumbled upon these verses in 2 Corinthians 13, the Lord challenged me on whether those desires were because I loved my current life or because I wanted Him. Then I decided I no longer wished to assume my desires for Him. I wanted to truly know if Jesus was my Lord or if I was just delusional. Therefore, I began testing myself thoroughly, no longer wishing to question God's place in my own life.

However, to test myself was no simple matter. Challenging my addictions, both seen and unseen, was a task that took countless hours of meditation. It required every ounce of strength to focus my mind on the Lord as I asked Him to strengthen my resolve to test myself.

For these tests made me question everything about myself, such as my use of money, my relational desires, my presuppositions, and my laziness. I fought to know whether God remained first in my life. My sinful nature questioned whether I really wished to know what remained hidden deep within myself, why it mattered, and the necessity of performing such tests.

Satan relentlessly bombarded me with questions, tempting me to stop in every moment, attempting to make me stumble. The incessant whines of demons and my own sinfulness constantly demanded me to stop. Regardless, the Lord strengthened me against these sinful doubts and reminded me time and time again that He was worth the pain and sacrifice.

There were many self-tests throughout the years. Although I am grateful that God gave me the strength to eventually overcome the trials, there were many times that I gave up, just to be picked up again. Oftentimes, it would seem as if I failed them, but God only used these moments to further remind me just how weak a person I am. Through friends, family, His Word, or just a momentary event, I was reminded that God was always there.

It was these tests that helped challenge my understanding of God. And it was these same tests that my Lord used to help strengthen me to be the person I am today. For these reasons, I have never stopped the practice of testing myself from that moment onward, and I continue to this day; it is a necessary practice to humble my pride.

However, the reason to test ourselves is not only to see if we have the resolve to overcome a challenge but also to find our own invisible sins that remain hidden within. For there are many blind spots we do not even know about in our lives. And if our known sins have so much power to sway our thoughts and interpretations of Scripture, just think of what our hidden ones can do while remaining unexposed.

13

Hidden Temptations

We are told that ignorance is bliss, but is it? For, as stated previously, the payment for our sins is death according to Romans 6:23. And Jesus explains how every word that is spoken will have to be accounted for after we perish in Matthew 12:36: "I tell you that every idle word that men speak, they will give account of it in the day of judgment."

Therefore, even if we remain ignorant of our sinfulness, the consequences of sin remain despite our lack of knowledge, often hurting ourselves and those around us. Then how can we continue to accept our own ignorance? Why do we not test and challenge our own presuppositions through the lens of Scripture?

Our presumptions can be much greater than we first imagined because we all have thoughts we assume are true. However, what if they are only partial truths? What if we believe they are true only because we have viewed them from one side and not the other?

There are times when we can believe our own practices are justified because of our freedom, but are they? Then why do we drink alcohol? Why do we get tattoos? Why do we play or watch certain sports, video games, movies, or TV shows?

For most of us, the reason is plain. It is simply because we want to. As illustrated in Proverbs 26:11, we are like dogs returning to eat our vomit. This explains why we rationalize our own sins away and quickly begin to point our fingers elsewhere, desiring to feel superior. This is also why, when we are called away from our own comfort zones and addictions, we are often filled with excuses and self-pity.

There are some that may argue that it is because such actions do not tempt them, and others who would argue that the Bible allows them the freedom to do such practices. Yet are those reasons alone good enough as Christ-followers? For if we remember from earlier, the Scriptures show we are free to practice all actions, but also that it is about what we *should* do rather than what we *can* do.

Have we so quickly forgotten what the Scriptures showed in Matthew 6:24 and Romans 6:16? If we are not doing an action for the Lord, then we are doing it for Satan and our sinful nature instead. Then why is it that when asked about our reasonings for doing such practices, the glory of God is rarely mentioned?

What reasons do we have for practicing such actions if they are for the Lord? We may hear about others who do these same actions to share the gospel or for other God-glorifying reasons. But what are our reasons for practicing them in our own lives?

For if our only reason we partake in these practices is because we are free to, then the obvious answer is that we are not doing them for the Lord. Because how can we do something for the Lord if all our arguments are based on freedom and self-desire? Therefore, even in the simplest of choices, we can see how we do most actions out of sinful desire rather than to be pleasing to our Lord and Savior.

It is easy to be enticed into believing that our actions are "okay" to do. However, in the same thought process, we have become slaves to Satan rather than to God through this ignorance. Because it is not "okay" to even practice the simplest of actions if it replaces our King with ourselves, as we are either servants of righteousness or of our sinfulness (Matthew 6:24).

For we are naturally sinful beings, and our tendency is to feed our own presumptions of right and wrong instead of challenging them. This is also why our preconceived thoughts and ideas easily sway our interpretations of Scripture unbeknownst to us. Because it requires less time and thought to interpret Scripture through our own lens rather than through the lens of Scripture itself.

Nevertheless, it is not correct to be ignorant just because it is easier. The need to identify our wrongful predispositions is vital to our health as Christians. For if we wish to follow Jesus, many times the greatest barrier is our own misguided interpretations of Scripture. We read one passage or book in the Bible and treat it separate from the rest.

Then let us test ourselves by asking questions that are important to helping us interpret Scripture properly: Who is speaking? Who is the audience? What are their perspectives? How would they understand the message back then? How does this interpretation fit with the rest of Scripture? We can use these questions as a guide to test our interpretations of Scripture.

However, we forget that many of these questions pertain to ourselves as well; we must consider how our presumptions can skew our own understandings. Do we believe more in the individual or community? Do we have tendencies more toward harshness or gentleness? How can our environments affect our own interpretations? How does our worldview align with the Bible?

For we learn many things passively through our surroundings. We can gain unknown tendencies from how our parents treated or mistreated us, our cultures, or even our choices of entertainment. And if we can determine how we have been influenced by our environments, we can ask how those influences compare to what God says in His Word.

One such example was when I thought about my social context while growing up. I grew up in a Chinese Church in America. However, both cultures constantly clashed with one another. The Chinese culture taught me to respect authority without question, that it was all about the community, and that love came from strict discipline. But the American culture taught me to think for myself, that it was all about me, and that love came from overabundant positivity.

This caused me to struggle constantly. Which teaching was right, and which was wrong? Because of these clashing ideologies, I tested myself against both. What did Scripture say about the individual, authority, and love? And it was only by the grace of God that He revealed to me it was both and neither. Both had some merits in Scripture, but neither was fully correct. What my environment taught was only partially true, teaching me to lean in one direction versus another. However, it was only God and His Word that could help me make sense of the contradicting ideologies of the world.

As we can see, the design of testing ourselves is to expose not only our known weaknesses but also the unknown ones. Therefore, if God and His Word are supposedly our guide, then why do we not also lower our own pride by testing against ourselves and previous notions before determining them to be true or false?

Would it not be wise to even test against our own biblical understandings, weighing between the arguments rooted in His Word? Should we not test against even our own presuppositions by challenging our beliefs and ideas? For it is easy to say when interpreting Scripture, "This is not what God meant." However, is that the actual truth, or do we only view it that way because we do not want what is plain to be true?

The most dangerous part of this problem is our misunderstanding of just how powerful our presumptions can be. For these preconceived notions have not only helped shape our thoughts and actions but can continue to do so even after we are made aware of their presence.

They lie deep within our sinful nature. Unexposed and unchallenged, they can continue to fester and control even the tiniest parts of our lives. Then, will we allow our old sinful nature to remain in control, or will we remember God has given us the strength to overcome even the toughest trials?

Yet one of the greatest pitfalls of testing ourselves is that we can end up testing the Lord instead. Because we are called to test ourselves, not to test God.

We are shown this when Jesus replied to Satan, saying, "Again, it is written, 'You shall not test the Lord, your God'" (Matthew 4:7). Then, we must ask ourselves whether our tests are being done to satisfy our sinful nature or to fight against it. Because even our prayers to God become tests against Him when we demand that His power be revealed and He do as we command.

For it is easy to read the stories of miraculous healing within Scripture and of God's power, only to desire it selfishly for our own gain. We have heard the stories of God granting power over Satan and his demons, of the separation of the Red Sea, of David and Goliath. We have heard of His grace and mercy through miraculous healings of leprosy and blindness. Yet we wonder why we have yet to be blessed with the same powers shown in these stories.

Our prayers seem to consistently fall on deaf ears when we request that God heal loved ones or ourselves. We ask God to prove Himself by demonstrating His power to us. But God does not have to prove anything to us.

Therefore, before testing ourselves, we must ask if the test is truly a test against our sinful natures or just a test against the Lord. Do our tests even fight against our addictions, or are they for self-gain? Do we test ourselves to feel good about our deeds, to pat ourselves on the back for doing "enough," or because we want God to be above all else in our lives?

For even in the most extreme practices, our hearts can be in the wrong. A good example of this is our understanding of the practice of "fasting." We talk about fasting as if it was another simple test, like not watching TV for a week or playing games for a month. Surely these are excellent tests to have in one's life to evaluate against sinful desire, but these are different from a biblical "fast."

Because "fasting," in Scripture, refers to an absence of food or drink, such as the case in Esther 4:16: "Go, gather together all the Jews who are present in Shushan, and fast for me, and neither eat nor drink three days, night or day. I and my maidens will also fast the same way. Then I will go in to the king, which is against the law; and if I perish, I perish."

Not eating or drinking was a declaration to God that they desired Him more than even the daily necessities of life. Their fasting was a plea to the Lord to help them discern His voice, because to be with God was more important than even life itself, and it was a recognition that God is the ultimate provider. It was no mere test against excessive desires but against the necessities of life itself. Yet even this extreme method of seeking the Lord can be done with the wrong heart mentality.

For, as shown by Jesus in Matthew 6:16, we are to not make it obvious that we are fasting: "Moreover when you fast, don't be like the hypocrites, with sad faces. For they disfigure their faces, that they may be seen by men to be fasting. Most certainly I tell you, they have received their reward."

Therefore, we should have practices that minimize the chance of sinful temptation caused by even the most extreme self-tests. We should be vigilant in deciphering if we are doing it to seek after the Lord or not.

So let us root out the evil within our lives, leaving no space unchecked or hidden. For by finding our own issues and problems, we can know where the enemy lies, and the enemy can no longer hide when fully revealed.

Let us start by first realizing what our sinful desires are, and then let us battle against them in order to tear down their strongholds within us. Because the identification of our addictions may be one issue, however, the battle against those addictions can sometimes feel like an entirely different tale.

14

Fleeing Addictions

Thankfully, in Scripture God teaches us many practical ways to deal with our addictions. However, it requires us to be alert and disciplined in our spiritual defense. For our presumptions can even sway how we deal with our sinful desires.

Many times, Satan deceives us, leading many, including myself, to believe there is no way to have victory over our sins. For example, while it is true that Jesus has already paid the ultimate price for our sins, this is but another piece of Scripture that Satan can use to deceive us. By taking accurate statements out of context, he can veil what is fully true. Because, as stated before, we need to have a wholistic biblical view.

Then why do we forget that even though God has paid the ultimate price for our sin, this does not mean our sins no longer have power while remaining in this world? Why did we forget that our sins still have great power to hurt ourselves and those around us when we remain apart from God?

For only if we remain steadfast and "love" God can He transform even the worst of our mistakes into the most beneficial, giving Him the glory, as shown in Romans 8:28. Are we then going to continue in our own ways, allowing our addictions to enslave and shackle our minds? Will we continue to allow our sins to hurt others and prevent them from seeing the glory and majesty of our God?

Therefore, just because we sin does not mean we must remain enslaved by sin. For our sins carry consequences and have negative effects on ourselves and those around us only as long as we remain apart from the Lord. They can only continue to hurt and bind us and others if unaddressed within our lives.

Let us remember God has given us a spirit of victory and not of defeat. As Philippians 4:13 says, "I can do all things through Christ, who strengthens me."

Therefore, let us be steadfast and remember that there is a way to have victory over any temptation. For even though we remain in our current sinful bodies in this world, God has also given us the tools necessary to help us continue the fight against our sinful natures. So, what are these tools that God gives us to deal with our temptations?

One of these tools is our practice of fleeing. In 2 Timothy 2:22, we are told to flee from sinful passions and pursue righteousness: "Flee from youthful lusts; but pursue righteousness, faith, love, and peace with those who call on the Lord out of a pure heart."

But what exactly does it mean to flee? Are we to physically run away from our addictions and attend marathons? Surely, it can include similar events, but the most obvious answer is that the fleeing mentioned refers to a mental battle rather than a physical one.

We need to run away from the thoughts of addiction. In practice, this can be done through a plethora of ways, whether through active thoughts or prevention. The specific action matters little, as long as it helps us to think of something other than the current temptation that has consumed our minds.

One way to flee from addictions, as previously mentioned, is through the practice of godly speech. Through the power of the Lord and intentionality, we can learn how to flee from our sin-filled thoughts. By speaking with the Holy Spirit and speaking against our sinful nature, we can learn how to prepare our mental defenses against the evil one. The goal is to get rid of the sinful thought completely when it arises. Therefore, we need only to change the topic from within.

One good example of this is being purposeful in prayer when tempted. However, if prayer alone is not enough, we can flee through other practices that force the mind to think elsewhere. Going out for a walk is another example, but if walking is not enough, then let us run. Even running a marathon is not out of the question. Whatever it takes to flee mentally from our sinful mindsets. Anything to change the topic that dwells within.

Nevertheless, one of the greatest pitfalls in attempting to flee from our immoral desires is being tricked by the evil one. There can be times when Satan fools us into believing that we are running away, when in reality, we have fallen into his trap again.

While being tempted, we recite passages of Scripture and plead with the Lord to take the desires and temptations away, screaming aloud within our heads. We shout out at God that we do not wish to desire such sin-filled things! Why then does this conversation usually end with our eventual failure? The simple answer is because we never fled to begin with.

When reflecting upon the desire to *not* perform a specific action, we have instead continued to linger on that same action. The same temptations remain because we are still in thought about the temptation itself. If we are told, "Do *not* open the door," is there not still a desire, tiny or not, to open the door? Even if previously unaware of the door's existence, have we not begun thinking of the door?

Therefore, whether we think of opening the door or not opening the door, the topic of the door still remains in our minds. Likewise, when we think about trying to *not* commit an addictive practice, we have instead continued to linger on the topic. This is the opposite of what we are trying to accomplish.

Because we are not told to ask God to remove every desire but to instead "pursue righteousness," as shown in the second part of 2 Timothy 2:22. Therefore, instead of thinking about what we should *not* do, we should think of what *to do* to flee sinful thoughts. This is how we can successfully apply the practice of mentally fleeing.

We can run away from our sin-filled thoughts by asking proactive questions geared toward changing the topic and getting our minds off our sinful temptations. What should I be doing as a Christ-follower instead of dwelling on this temptation? How can I accomplish this goal? Proactive questions like these can help us mitigate the heat of temptation by quickly changing the topic matter at hand. By changing our mindset of self-loathing into productive thoughts rooted in actionable ideas, we can turn our gaze from temptation back to the Lord.

Yet another way to practice fleeing our addictive desires besides godly speech is through prevention. A good example of this is the practice of setting guardrails. Essentially, the idea is to set barriers within our lives that can help dissuade the mind from even being tempted to begin with.

Conceptually, it is like running away from the battle before it even begins. This practice can include things such as placing parental locks on our electronic devices or having weekly accountability meetings with another Christ-follower. The greater the barrier, the harder it is to jump past. Therefore, the practices of fleeing through godly speech and guardrails are essential in our fight against sinful temptations.

However, this tool is not only limited to lustful desires because the training of one's mind to focus on Christ is useful in the fight against any sinful temptation, whether it is against our pride or lack of joy in Christ.

Hence, the same reasons to flee mentally from our sinfulness are also why we are warned of the dangers of idleness and laziness throughout Scripture. Because idleness is the brain *not* being active in fleeing temptations.

As shown in 2 Thessalonians 3:10-13, being lazy equates to letting our guard down and walking in rebellion:

> For even when we were with you, we commanded you this: "If anyone will not work, neither let him eat." For we hear of some who walk among you in rebellion, who don't work at all, but are busybodies. Now those who are that way, we command and exhort in the Lord Jesus Christ, that with quietness they work, and eat their own bread. But you, brothers, don't be weary in doing well.

It is so dangerous that the apostles even command us in 2 Thessalonians 3:14 to stay away from fellow Christians who continue their path of idleness and "rebellion" and refuse to work. Because dwelling with an idle and lazy person is the same as being unequally yoked with non-believers. As verse 14 says, "If any man doesn't obey our word in this letter, note that man, that you have no company with him, to the end that he may be ashamed."

Some may ask, "What is the difference between 'laziness' and 'rest'?" It is simple. The purpose of "rest" is to allow time to recover from mental and physical fatigue when dealing with the world, while remaining vigilant in the Lord. However, "idleness" numbs the mind from all thoughts and actions of the Lord, causing us to dwell on our own wants and desires. For Exodus 33:14 shows that only through God can rest occur: "He said, 'My presence will go with you, and I will give you rest.'"

In other words, rest keeps God at the forefront of our minds while realizing our mortal bodies need time to recover. Yet idleness and laziness ignore God even when He calls us to action. Therefore, even in our times of rest we are called to have God first and foremost in our hearts, or else our "rest" is but idleness and laziness.

However, many of us have remained torn from within despite having understood all these things. While these practices against sinful addictions can be of great help in dealing with urges and desires, it can still continue to feel as if something remains lacking. Whether we apply guardrails through the addition of parental locks on electronic devices, setting up accountability groups, or actively fleeing through prayer and distractions, we can continue to feel distressed.

Sometimes, even with our current disciplines, the weariness of sin may continue to take its toll on us. It can feel like there is no reprieve from the battle. But we have only fallen into another one of Satan's many deceits.

15

Recognition Vs. Understanding

Although many of us recognize we must flee from sinful desires and continue in our fight against Satan, our battle against sinful desires can seem incomplete at times.

Seeing countless Christians seemingly defeated by the lies of Satan, we have watched as brothers, sisters, and spiritual leaders have fallen one after another, addictions in plain view. There are times when it can feel as if everything is a lie, as if our battle against sin is meaningless. The mental toll of spiritual warfare can almost feel unbearable at times.

What is missing? How can it be possible for God's yoke to feel light when the burden of fighting our addictions is so heavy? Why can it feel as if our sinful nature unceasingly screams out from within? This feeling can be caused by our false presumptions yet again.

Sometimes, due to our sinful nature, we can recognize something is true but reject its truth because it exposes our weaknesses. Our sinful nature can prevent us from fully understanding what is plain in Scripture by making it complex and convoluted to justify our own actions. We can end up doubting what is true when circumstances do not work out the way we expected. Instead of pushing forward, we can end up going back to our old ways.

This sickness occurs mainly when we think we have implemented Scripture in our lives, yet in reality have only stepped in halfway. It's similar to trying out new foods; we can sometimes have a preconceived notion of a food tasting horrible and continue feeding into that notion before even really trying it. We can end up swallowing something before allowing our tongues to touch and taste it.

Likewise, there are times we can be told an idea and recognize its importance, but not fully believe in it because we had made up our minds previously. We can fool ourselves into thinking that we fully understand something when, in reality, our understanding is distorted by our stubbornness. These presumptions can then end up corrupting our understanding of Scripture.

For example, we previously talked about how joy and hate are both needed in our lives as long as they are viewed correctly through the lens of Scripture, and we discussed how we are to "abhor" sin (per Romans 12:9). Specifically, the Greek word for "abhor" is "apostugeó," which means to detest utterly. It is easy enough for us to recognize that we should not continue to sin. However, do we hate or detest utterly our sinful practices?

Because I question if we really believe in the true gravity of our sinful desires. For whenever many of us stumble into the pitfalls of our addictions, we seem keener on reminding ourselves of grace and mercy instead of figuring out a way to prevent the addictive action from happening again.

In my struggle with my addictions of lust, I used many spiritual practices to attempt fleeing from sinful temptations, but it felt like it was never enough. Though there were periods when even months and years would pass without relapse of my old sinful practices, it felt as if I was always stuck at war in the same place.

It felt as if the burdens of my addictions would never lessen. The fights were tedious and grueling, and I grew exhausted throughout the years. To fight my sinful nature was to be at constant battle with myself. It felt as if no matter how hard I fought against Satan and my inner desire, I could never increase my natural desires for what God wanted.

It felt like there was something missing in my life. There had to be a better way to deal with my addictions. I wanted a heart mentality that desired the Lord over all else at all times. It was in these thoughts that God challenged me, reminding me of the need to abhor sin.

I questioned my own thoughts of hating sin and pondered the old church practice of self-flagellation, which is physically beating oneself to fight against the addictions of sin. Many in the modern church would frown upon this extreme practice. However, were those who used to practice these acts of brutal beatings just crazy back then? Did this practice have no merit?

My immediate thought was that the people who used to practice self-flagellation were insane. My second thought was that there was no point in such a harmful practice. However, it was then that I sought to challenge my inherent beliefs.

>I was reminded of Matthew 5:29-30:
>
>If your right eye causes you to stumble, pluck it out and throw it away from you. For it is more profitable for you that one of your members should perish, than for your whole body to be cast into Gehenna. If your right hand causes you to stumble, cut it off, and throw it away from you. For it is more profitable for you that one of your members should perish, than for your whole body to be cast into Gehenna.

In this passage, Jesus reminded His listeners of the detriments of sin. He explained how it would be better for them to lose a hand or an eye than to continue in sin and be thrown into hell. Yet why did I quickly dismiss this claim by explaining that Jesus was just using hyperbole and exaggeration? Why did I rationalize within myself that there is no way our Lord would wish for the removal of body parts in exchange for our sins? Did I truly hate my sins if I was not willing to punish them in my own life?

Did I forget Romans 6:23, that the payment of my sin is death? Is death less severe than losing an eye or a limb? Of course not. I had forgotten that sin is no simple matter. Sin is, in essence, a mutiny against God, and the only punishment suited for such a mutiny is death. It is only through the self-sacrifice and perfect grace of Jesus, God Almighty, that we could be redeemed of our sins. Yet I wished to rationalize how removing a limb or an eye was too severe?

However, I wondered if this practice of limb removal was wise. For while there were valid arguments for the eventual removal of limbs, I knew the temptations of our sinful nature would still remain even with the removal of every body part. The largest problem with this practice of removing limbs lay within its limitations rather than its concepts. We are limited by the number of body parts we have. Therefore, the harsh reality is that there are simply not enough body parts to remove to dissuade us from our sinful desires.

These reasons made the act of removing body parts to be extremely limited in practice. For I knew of many instances where a person could be left with a permanent loss of limbs without any concrete solution for their continued sinful actions.

However, the justifications were now clear with self-flagellation. For even though this act of beating oneself was a harsh punishment similar to the removal of one's limbs, it was not limited. It could be implemented indefinitely rather than a set number of times. However, I still remained unclear on how this practice would help in my walk with Christ.

I thought about the similarities and differences between the practices of guardrails and self-flagellation. They seemed similar enough on the surface. Both practices were about adding defenses meant to dissuade from addictions, but I thought about how the implementation of self-flagellation would be a much greater dissuasion for my sinful addictions.

Why would I continue watching pornographic materials if I knew the pain that it would cause later? I wondered why physically beating myself would dissuade me from the sinful act. This led me to realize that it was because the consequences of pain outweighed the pleasures of the act.

Therefore, it soon became clear in my mind. The answer to my continued frustration was simple. I had been treating my sins too lightly. I had been making too many excuses for myself by using God's grace and mercy as a crutch to overlook my sinfulness.

RECOGNITION VS. UNDERSTANDING 131

All I needed was for my mind to naturally think of the consequences when desiring to do a sinful action. Self-flagellation was the answer they came up with in the past. However, I realized that self-flagellation was just one practice. God helped me see that I could simply identify a repeatable consequence that was harsh enough to dissuade from the sinful act and have enough determination to enforce it. In other words, through the practice of adding harsh consequences, God could transform my views and desires.

After realizing my false presumptions, I quickly thought of a harsh enough punishment that would help me think of my sins differently. In order to fight against the action of viewing pornographic materials, I quickly began to think of harsh enough consequences that would heavily dissuade me from the sinful act. It is then I decided that if I was to watch any pornographic materials that I would fast for a week.

I believed that losing my ability to eat food would be a great enough dissuasion to my temptations. Because the practice not only could help me run away from the temptation but also concurrently pursue righteousness. Hence, the fasting process was not only a deterrent to my lustful temptations, but it was also a wise practice to help me focus my mind back on the Lord.

Yet, the time arose when I stumbled once more from temptation. It was then that Satan also tempted me to not enact my self-punishment. This is when God quickly reminded me of the severity of my sin. I was reminded that the most important part of the practice of harsh punishments was not to understand how to implement the practice but to enforce the punishment when required.

Otherwise, I would know deep down that the punishment was but a lie, and that would defeat the entire purpose. I knew that a rule had no power unless enforced. Therefore, for this to work, I had to view sin through a godly lens. I had to see it for what it truly is, a disgusting part of my life that God sees no beauty in. For it is not the sin itself that has beauty, but rather the grace and mercy required to redeem us of that sin that is beautiful.

Soon after realizing these things, I began my self-punishment. It was not a fun week, and there were even times that I had to modify or completely overhaul this punishment. One example was a simple change in my fasting time when I extended the punishment further by days. But funny enough, this is when I realized something fundamental had changed inside me. For after the punishment, my mind would only dwell upon the punishments when I was tempted again in the future.

The harsh punishment helped focus my mind on the consequences of losing food in exchange for momentary pleasure. Due to the cons remaining greater than the pros, my mind would naturally think of the consequences first when being tempted to sin in the future.

I was no longer fatigued by the active battles between my old and new life. My brain began to see sin for what it actually was. I began to only see the displeasure of my sinful nature rather than the pleasure. Yet there may be some who still do not see how the practice of adding self-punishments is any different from the other practices we perform, like actively fleeing addictions or setting up guardrails.

Then, let us imagine three men. These three men were no ordinary men, for all three had a great desire to jump off a certain mountain cliff. Their desire was no simple temptation, for they wished to jump without any equipment due to their lust for adrenaline rushes.

For even though they all knew of the dangers, and that jumping meant certain death, they fantasized of the day that they could finally fulfill their dreams. The scariest part yet is that every day, they were forced to pass by this mountain cliff.

When the first man passed by the cliffside, he knew that he would have to sway his mind away from thinking of the cliffside to prevent himself from jumping. For he knew that death would surely come if he did not fight his temptations, but the desire still remained.

Therefore, in order to prevent himself from jumping, he implemented the idea of fleeing mentally. While passing the steep mountainside, he began to look at his feet, trying to distract his mind from the cliff. But in the end, he had a momentary lapse of judgment and glanced up. Upon seeing the beauty of the cliff, he was again reminded of his desire to jump and quickly leapt to his death.

Then came the second man, who also had the same great temptation to jump off the mountainside. He also implemented the same practice as the first man. However, when staring at his feet, he decided that it was not enough to just look away when tempted by the cliffside.

He thought to himself that he needed something more to defend himself from his great desire. Therefore, the second man built a guardrail beside the cliff. He prided himself on how the railing would surely be enough to prevent his temptations. But when the man looked up one day and saw the beauty of the mountainside, he, too, ran toward it, simply climbing over his affixed railing, and eventually he jumped to his death like the first man.

Yet there remained one last man. This third man also practiced the same defenses against temptation as the first two men. Yet, this man was different. For he loved his wife and children at home and did not wish to depart from them. Therefore, he did not even want to chance being overcome by his temptations. For he knew that he, too, would eventually be forced to pass the steep mountain cliffs.

He knew the eventual consequence of his own temptations, that he could have times of weakness, leading to a momentary lapse of judgment. He knew that there was a possibility of death if he were to look up from his feet and climb over his guardrail when passing by the cliffside.

Therefore, in order to make sure he did not die, he did what no other man before him had done. In order to protect himself, he did everything he could possibly think of. This man built a wall by the mountainside, making it so high that the cliff was no longer visible. He electrified the guardrails so that he would never dare to touch the walls, for he wanted to make sure that he would never jump off the cliff.

However, he, too, was eventually tempted while passing the steep mountainside. He attempted to jump as well, but something strange happened. Instead of jumping from the cliffside, he walked away alive and healthy. For when trying to get over the barriers, they burned him. No matter how hard he tried, he could not muster enough willpower to fight the pain of crossing the electrified guardrails. And from then on, when thinking about the cliffside, he was instead reminded only of the painful experience of attempting to cross.

Let us ask then, which of these three men are we most like? Are we more like the first or second man who only set up one or two methods to protect themselves from the cliffside? Do we attempt to fight against our sins halfheartedly? Do we pat ourselves on the back for trying when failing? Is it a God-centered heart mentality to quit our pursuits of righteousness? Rather than gain greater urgency, many times we make excuses for ourselves about why we remain chained to our sinful desires.

Then why is it so hard to be more like the third man who refused to make excuses for himself? It is because our presumption of thinking we have tried enough can sometimes be the difference between recognizing an idea versus understanding it. For the third man did not only acknowledge a simple need to abhor temptation but fully understood what it meant, doing whatever was necessary to deal with his problems.

We often wonder why we continue to struggle with certain addictive actions, even after many years. There are many of us who agree with the negative reinforcement of disciplining children shown in Proverbs 13:24, who remember God's punishment of King David for his sins of adultery and murder in 2 Samuel 12:13-15, and who remember when Jesus overturned the tables within the synagogues in Matthew 21:12-13 and Mark 11:15-18.

But why is it when viewing our own sins that we tread so lightly? In the few moments of hearing that our sin is hated by the Lord, why do we instead quickly remind ourselves of God's enormous grace? Did we forget about His wrath toward the city of Sodom and Gomorrah in Genesis 19? Were they not destroyed for their rampant, unrepentant sin?

We presume that we have a good understanding of sin within our own lives but have ended up deceived by our own desires for comfort. We have heard of the vileness of sin yet have only half-heartedly tried to address it. Using the cross as a crutch, we have continued on in our filthy ways.

For not only is it possible for us to understand God's wrath toward sin, but it is also possible to naturally desire a life that pleases Him. It is possible to realize that we have not been harsh enough on our sins, to realize the power that God has given us over our old selves, to desire Him above all, and in the end be told, "Well done, good and faithful servant" (Matthew 25:21).

We rationalize our issues as if we deserve to be redeemed, and we simultaneously take for granted the grace required to forgive our sins. We have heard of the gravity of sin, that it is detestable. Yet we continue in our unwillingness to address sin, even when everything is consumed and destroyed in its wake.

While glancing away from the nails pierced through the hands of Jesus and the thorns entrenched on His head, we point at the cross. We proclaim grace and mercy, yet do not dare look at our sins upon that cross, our sins mounted on His head and piercing His feet. It is time for us to look up! Gaze upon what was paid for you and me. Let us never forget that the redemption of our sinful nature was bought through an enormous sacrifice.

Let us not forget that it is our sin that put Jesus on the cross. Let us not forget our old smell of death and decay. For we were only walking dead. From death to life, we were raised up. Yet, we easily forget what was paid. We forget that our sins are disgusting to the Lord. We forget how it harms those around us and ourselves, how it can infect everything it touches.

We cower and hide behind reasons and excuses. We continue down the path of destruction when it is those very ways that cause us pain. By hiding our problems and pretending they are not there, we have ignored the Lord for far too long.

16

Promise Keeper

We tend to make light of sin. We point at the visible addictions of others so that we do not have to focus on our own issues. We talk about how others need to deal with their sins without giving practical ways or illustrations, as if it was some simple thing. But if we were being honest with ourselves, we would not talk of temptation and lust with such simplicity.

Because truthfully, it is no simple task to deal with addictions. It takes every ounce of our willpower to even attempt to address them, and many of us would rather point fingers than look in the mirror, for the emotions that cloud our judgments also consume us.

Many times, we are just exhausted. Filled with pain, anger, and bitterness, we wish to repay others and cause the same feelings that have hurt us so much. We remember God's promises and mercy, yet in our moment of frustration, nothing matters. We lash out in anger at anyone, even God, just to feel a semblance of relief.

For many of us have felt the emotional taxation of living in this world. We have prayed with fierce intensity just to be given the silent treatment from God. We have struggled for far too long while watching others who dwell in evil prosper. We can end up jaded with the world. We can grow tired of doing things for the right reasons and feel like enough is enough.

But what if I told you that this feeling was another way that God was speaking to us? For we have discussed how dealing with our addictions leads us to desire our Lord. Yet we often forget why the desire itself even manifests.

For not only did our God defeat sin and death on the cross, He is also the promise keeper. Hebrews 10:23 says, "Let us hold fast the confession of our hope without wavering; for he who promised is faithful."

Then, if we believe God is faithful, all we must do is trust in His promises. Because He who always remains faithful promises to always give us whatever we desire if we truly seek after Him: "If you remain in me, and my words remain in you, you will ask whatever you desire, and it will be done for you" (John 15:7).

In other words, the practices of godly speech, testing ourselves, and self-punishments are merely examples of how our desires can manifest for the Lord. But the true reason why we can trust that the desire will appear is because our God promises to make it happen.

Therefore, we can know that we are following His will when our emotional desires naturally seek after Him because God promises to give us the desires of our heart if they are of Him. Our desires for God's way over our own are God's way of reminding us that He is pleased with us. These desires are a way to confirm our walks with Christ.

However, just as we can gain those stronger desires for the Lord, we can also lack a desire for Him because God is also willing to let us go our way if we continue to be hard-headed and ignore His calling, as shown in Romans 1:24: "Therefore God also gave them up in the lusts of their hearts to uncleanness, that their bodies should be dishonored among themselves."

In other words, just as a desire for God is His way of telling us we are on the right path, the lack of desire for God's way over our temptations is His warning to us. Because to feel no desire for our Lord's will is the "canary in the coal mine," in a manner of speaking. For if we continue to ignore our Lord as He calls to us, He will, in turn, allow us to do as we please.

It's like a father who screamed desperately in an open field for his children to come home; the children who wished to come home ran toward his voice. And as they came closer, the father's voice became louder and clearer. But as for the children who ran from the call, ignoring his pleas, the father's voice soon became quieter and quieter, eventually becoming too silent to hear.

Likewise, just as the father screamed desperately for his children, our Father in Heaven continues to call out to us, pleading for us to return home. Understanding our feelings of desire is one more tool that can help us hear the Lord's voice. These feelings are the gauge of how close we are to God. They are His way of calling out to us. God uses our emotional desires for Him to tell us whether we are closer to Him or further from Him. Yet we can end up believing that God no longer beckons to us when we have gone our own way for too long.

Therefore, even if it may feel as if we are holding on by a thread, even if our bodies grow weary from the pain, even if it may feel like we will die in doing so, we must pull ourselves up. We must run back to our Lord. For emotions are a powerful thing, a trait that God blesses us with in order to help motivate our efforts. Yet, when abused, they are just as powerful at blinding us. For those emotions are the same tools that the deceiver uses to make us lose control, again ensnaring us back in our old ways.

And at some point, if we continue in our hard-headedness, ignoring God's pleas to turn back to Him, we will no longer be able to hear His call. We will lack all desire to seek Him over our own ways. Only silence will remain. Therefore, if we lack the desire to do our Lord's will, we should take great heed, for God is telling us that we are going the wrong way.

Like driving on ice, we need traction in order to drive straight. Our focus on God is that traction. When ignored, it is easy to slip off the path and be overcome by anything lying in wait.

We may try to argue and say that we have good reasons for dwelling in our sinful mentalities, claiming that it is because of health reasons, painful events, personality types, or someone else's actions. However, these are but further lies and half-truths of the devil. For there is always a way to conquer our temptations, and we have no excuse to continue in our sinfulness, regardless of how we feel. For God knew that we would fail in our own ways, and He has already made a way.

Because our God is a promise keeper, and He promises to always make a way. Therefore, we can remain confident that we will never be tempted beyond what we can handle. As 1 Corinthians 10:13 says, "No temptation has taken you except what is common to man. God is faithful, who will not allow you to be tempted above what you are able, but will with the temptation also make the way of escape, that you may be able to endure it."

In other words, despite sometimes feeling hopeless and overcome by the situation, there is always a way out. God has already prepared a way to deal with any challenge that our current temptations may throw at us. Regardless of whether this preparation is through the people He has already placed in our lives, our knowledge, or something else, we have already been given the tools necessary to deal with any temptation we currently face.

We can end up blaming God for not fulfilling His promise to give us the desires of our heart. Yet we often do not realize that He didn't grant us our desires because we never truly sought after Him all along. Because God only promises to give us the desires of our heart if we "remain in" Him (John 15:7).

We can lie down and complain about our temptations, yet when called to action, never take the steps necessary to fight against these sinful ways. God's call may only remain as mere thoughts and theories trapped within our minds, lacking any real intention on our part to implement them.

Just like the saying goes, we can end up looking at the glass half full or half empty. For if we remain in our sinfulness, even if the cup were to be filled to the brim, we would always find fault, complaining that the cup was too full or likely to spill.

But if we remain in Christ, even if the cup were to be completely dry, we would still find joy. For we would know that the water comes not from the cup but from the overflowing Spring of Life within us. John 4:14 says, "But whoever drinks of the water that I will give him will never thirst again; but the water that I will give him will become in him a well of water springing up to eternal life."

In other words, the true reason we can sometimes feel this way is because ultimately, regardless of how much knowledge we gain, how many theories we create, and how many new resolutions we make, the brutal truth is that we just need to stop. We need to stop making excuses and start applying God's Word in our lives.

For there are an infinite number of excuses that Satan and our own minds can create to explain why we should wait longer. And the reason many of us feel drained and overwhelmed, having no desire for the Lord, is because for far too long we have ignored His calling to us.

17

"Christian" in Name Alone

There are some who will remain in denial even after reading up to this point. In their stubbornness, they only argue further, claiming that they are free to do anything their sinful hearts desire for they have been redeemed. They recite verses like 1 John 5:13, "These things I have written to you who believe in the name of the Son of God, that you may know that you have eternal life, and that you may continue to believe in the name of the Son of God."

But they forget that Scripture should be viewed in its entirety rather than as a single verse, that the first part of 1 John 5:13 says, "These things that I have written to you." Therefore, we are only to be confident in our salvation if the things "written" in 1 John match with our own lives. Then, what are the things that the apostle John wrote in 1 John to describe those who should and should not be confident in their salvation?

In 1 John 2:3-4, he tells us that those who keep God's commandments are of God and those who do not are mere liars if claiming to be of God. In 1 John 2:15-16, the apostle John states that if we love the world, then God is not in us. We are told in 1 John 3:6 that no one that is of God continues in their sinful addictions. Therefore, we should have no confidence in our salvation if we continue in our own sinful desires, and we should only be confident in our salvation if our lives reflect what the Lord desires.

Then is it not insulting to ignore God's voice and still expect Him to listen to us when it best suits us? Let me ask, would we continue to go out of our way for those who only intend to abuse and misuse us? Likewise, how dare we expect God to lower Himself before us as if He were some type of personal wish-granting machine?

For these same decisions of defiance are why many of us should be wary of boldly claiming we are "Christians," since the title "Christian" means to follow Christ. It was a title given only to those whose lifestyles mimicked Jesus (Acts 11:26).

Yet when we choose our own ways over His way, then in no way, shape, or form, are we *following* Christ. I dare not say which of us have or have not been saved, for only the Lord knows this truth (1 Corinthians 4:1-5). But what does our Savior have to say to those of us who wish to continue with our bold claims of discipleship while ignoring His way and choosing our own instead?

It is only befitting then that we now come full circle to what was referenced when we first began this journey. For as we remember in Luke 14:26-33, we were shown what the requirements of being a disciple of Jesus are. We were shown that we must be willing to reject everything, including our own lives, to follow Him.

It is right after this extensive list of requirements that Jesus explained why the requirements set for being God's disciple are so harsh. In Luke 14:33-35, Jesus says, "So therefore whoever of you who doesn't renounce all that he has, he can't be my disciple. Salt is good, but if the salt becomes flat and tasteless, with what do you season it? It is fit neither for the soil nor for the manure pile. It is thrown out. He who has ears to hear, let him hear."

It is at this point that Jesus described those who claimed to be His disciples yet refused to live lives in accordance with that claim. He illustrated the usefulness of those who claim the title of "Christian" yet refuse to address their sinful addictions. Jesus explained how these people are less useful than dung, a salt that has lost its saltiness. For what purpose does salt have if it loses its intended design?

Likewise, what use is there for a Christian who does not actively follow Christ? Less than poop, according to Jesus. For not only would we then be liars, but we would also be tainting the very definition of what a Christian is. We would be polluting how others view God.

Therefore, we should not be surprised by the inevitable consequences if we wish to continue in our own ways and deny our King. These consequences may even entail being removed from the fellowship of our brothers and sisters in Christ. For we are called as Christians to not associate with those who claim to be of God yet remain consumed by their sinful addictions as Paul teaches in 1 Corinthians 5:11: "But as it is, I wrote to you not to associate with anyone who is called a brother who is a sexual sinner, or covetous, or an idolater, or a slanderer, or a drunkard, or an extortioner. Don't even eat with such a person."

And we are commanded to do this in the hope that those who are consumed by their addictions would repent and turn back from the destruction of their sinful ways. As 1 Corinthians 5:5 explains, you "are to deliver such a one to Satan for the destruction of the flesh, that the spirit may be saved in the day of the Lord Jesus."

Because we are not called to judge those outside the church but to judge those within the church: "For what have I to do with also judging those who are outside? Don't you judge those who are within? But those who are outside, God judges. 'Put away the wicked man from among yourselves'" (1 Corinthians 5:12-13).

For anyone who dares to claim the title of "Christian" yet refuses to follow Christ and His commands is using His name in vain. Therefore, let us not continue in our own ways with sinful addictions. Let us not push away those who earnestly seek after salvation from finding our God, our Lord, our Savior. Let us instead be the light in this world as God designed us to be, a shining beacon of God's love for others.

For what does it matter if we understand our freedoms under Christ or have all understanding of what Scripture says? Why does any of it matter if it only ends with our own hypocrisy? We may laugh at those who claim to be of Jesus when they fail to understand their freedoms in Christ. We laugh at the ridiculous, illogical rules that they make for themselves, mocking and shaking our heads in disagreement.

We may discuss how silly it is for certain communities to not accept electricity and modern attire. We say that they are foolishly bound by "old fashioned" rules, with little to no reasoning. We argue about how they make idols of their rules and are enslaved by their own illogical fallacies. Yet what about us who know our freedoms?

If we understand our freedoms, do our lives then reflect that knowledge? Or do we only abuse those very freedoms for sinful gain and fill our lives with other idols? Because when our arguments are rooted in self, our freedoms have only become shackles of Satan. If we do everything our sinful hearts desire, while excusing our lack of Scripture meditation and prayer, are we not then just the same as those whom we mock? Have not our freedoms become idols we use as an excuse for doing only what we please?

Then let us ask ourselves in all genuineness: Is it a heart for the Lord that we seek? Because sometimes we may understand the logical reasoning behind how and why something works, yet our lives demonstrate that we believe otherwise. For we may proclaim that we wish for God to give us a desire for Him, yet when we are given the opportunity to change, time and time again, we continue to choose only our own path.

If we are told by Jesus that lusting after another is the same as committing adultery in Matthew 5:28, then why are we okay with dating practices that tempt us for years, lusting after others with no determination for marriage? Why do we defile our bodies with inappropriate relationships and indulge in places of sensual pleasures designed to bring us further into sin?

We desire everything that pleases us in romantic relationships, from intimacy to companionship to the "fun" times. Yet we refuse to fully commit ourselves to another because we know there will be bad times when they act against our ideals, when they cheat, lie, steal, and do as they please.

If we are shown in His Word that the love of money is the root of many sins in 1 Timothy 6:10, then why are we never content with what we already have? "For the love of money is a root of all kinds of evil. Some have been led astray from the faith in their greed, and have pierced themselves through with many sorrows."

For if we cannot be satisfied now with what we already have, what makes us think that having more of what we already have will fill our desire? What is the purpose of taking out loans and going into debt for things we cannot afford when Scripture warns us of the dangers of loans? Proverbs 22:7 explains that the borrower is bound to the lender: "The rich rule over the poor. The borrower is servant to the lender."

Is it truly God that guides our decisions or just the sinful indulgence of our temptations? Have we become like the Israelites who prostituted themselves before a golden calf while waiting for the Lord (Exodus 32:8)? Have we been dancing before our freedoms, whoring ourselves before them in drunken nakedness?

Because it is not a matter of forcing ourselves into self-discipline for the pure sake of self-betterment. For that, too, remains a sin. It is about forcing ourselves to fight against our sinful natures because our desire should not be for ourselves but to be a people after God's own heart. It is about our decision to choose the Lord over all else.

Because our God is always speaking to us. Even in the silence His words are known, but it is up to us to listen and understand when He speaks. For our pleasures rooted in sinful desires are not of true benefit to us. They are just further lies from Satan to hold us back from being of any value in the hidden battle that rages.

For we are not at war with people or each other. We are in a spiritual war. Therefore, we must take every thought captive. As 2 Corinthians 10:3-5 says, "For though we walk in the flesh, we don't wage war according to the flesh; for the weapons of our warfare are not of the flesh, but mighty before God to the throwing down of strongholds, throwing down imaginations and every high thing that is exalted against the knowledge of God, and bringing every thought into captivity to the obedience of Christ."

18

A New Era to Come

It is here that we can hopefully now see how our presumptions and sinful natures have run far deeper than we had first thought. Hopefully, God has now opened our eyes, and we have seen how our hearts have been hardened and twisted with false predispositions.

Then this leaves us with a final consideration that can be summed up with one word: "Repentance." Are we willing to repent of our sinful ways? Are we willing to implement all the tools God has given in order to turn back to Him and fight against our shortcomings?

For it is one thing to recognize and understand how we have fallen short of following Christ; it is another thing to see how we can change our ways. Yet it all remains worthless without a desire for our Lord. All of our knowledge and understanding is meaningless if we only continue in our own ways and refuse to turn back to our Lord and pursue Him above all else.

In Matthew 3:8-9, John the Baptist proclaimed, "Therefore bring forth fruit worthy of repentance! Don't think to yourselves, 'We have Abraham for our father,' for I tell you that God is able to raise up children to Abraham from these stones."

His message was clear. He told them to repent of their ways. He showed in verse 8 that repentance has actions that flow from a changed heart mentality, and he also made a dire warning in verse 9.

For back then, the Israelites assumed they were safe from the condemnation of the Lord because their lineage stemmed from Abraham. However, John the Baptist clearly told them they should not assume they were safe because of their lineage. In other words, we should not be so sure of ourselves and our salvation if there remains no fruit that stems from our so called "repentance."

Consistently, throughout Scripture, we are told that the word "repent" means to "turn again" or reverse from our previous ways, such as in Acts 3:19, "Repent therefore, and turn again, that your sins may be blotted out, so that there may come times of refreshing from the presence of the Lord."

God even gives us examples of this through the lives described in Scripture. For instance, through the tax collector Zacchaeus, we are shown that repentance to God is not just some simple acknowledgment of wrongdoing but a complete life change.

For when Zacchaeus realized his sinfulness in front of Jesus, he gave four times the amount back to those he had previously defrauded and half of his entire estate to the poor. Luke 19:8 says, "Zacchaeus stood and said to the Lord, 'Behold, Lord, half of my goods I give to the poor. If I have wrongfully exacted anything of anyone, I restore four times as much.'"

Some would call this act "crazy," and others would say it is "insanity." Yet it is this very insanity for our Lord, our King, that is called "repentance." Yet what does that word "repentance" mean in our own lives?

Does it mean to flaunt our freedoms? Does it mean we can do as we please? Does it mean we should state a simple apology? Because repentance is not a mere recognition of guilt. To repent is to completely turn around, implementing ways to prevent our mistakes from happening again. Therefore, if we continue our attempts at quickly hiding and ignoring sinful mistakes, we could never be described as "repentant."

Do we dare to continue pleading for forgiveness before our King when we refuse to change our ways? Do we expect Him to reveal Himself to us when we only see Him as a tool? For He is no simple fool!

He is Alpha and Omega! He is Jehovah Jireh, the ultimate provider! He is Jehovah Rapha, the ultimate healer! He is Jehovah Shammah, the One who always remains present! He is Jehovah Raah, the ultimate guide and shepherd, and

He is the only One who is worthy of all praise! "Holy, holy, holy is the Lord God, the Almighty, who was and who is and who is to come!" (Revelation 4:8).

Then will we, too, be the same as those who mock our God? Will we continue to be salt that has lost its saltiness, worth less than dung? Will we continue to run in fear of the world while our King watches? Will we continue to allow the fear of pain, suffering, death, and disease to guide our ways? Will we allow Satan to continue using us like puppets on a string?

Though I do not know your answer, I, for one, will no longer continue to run. I will no longer flee from His calling. I will no longer continue to be controlled by the evil one and allow Satan to rule over my life. For I am a Christian. I am a Christ-follower, and my desire is for my King. For He is King of all kings, and He is worthy.

For I, too, like Jonah fleeing from the Lord's calling, have fled for far too long, avoiding what God has called me to do. For I fear what will come of this very written work as it spreads. I fear this world and what will become of my life. I fear the masses and what they may do to me.

I fear like the apostle Peter who denied Jesus three times while running for his life. I fear the ones who once crucified my Lord. I fear the mockery and jeering that Noah experienced as he built the ark. I fear the pain and suffering of Job when all was taken from him, realizing that Satan may cause great harm to my friends and family.

Yet I fear my King more. For Jesus tells us whom we should truly fear in Matthew 10:28: "Don't be afraid of those who kill the body, but are not able to kill the soul. Rather, fear him who is able to destroy both soul and body in Gehenna."

Then why should I fear Satan or the world when all they may do is destroy my physical body? What power do demons hold over me compared to my God who has conquered death? For my God is not so weak as to only be able to destroy my physical body; He can destroy my spiritual self as well. Did I forget Proverbs 1:7, that the "fear of Yahweh is the beginning of knowledge"?

For it is this very fear of my Lord and Savior that pushes me onward. I fear more of what I will see before the judgment seat of Christ. I fear the gaze of my King looking down upon me in sadness and disappointment. I fear hearing His woeful words asking me why I ran away from everything except my old self. I fear living a life without my Savior. I fear making a mockery of the sacrifice my Lord made on the cross for you and me, as my sins lay upon His head as a crown of thorns.

Because truthfully, my eyes were clouded for far too long. Consumed by my hidden wants and desires, those lying within the darkness deceived me. But it is now the time to leave behind all my excuses. It is time to unshackle myself from Satan and come back to my Lord.

Likewise, will you also join me in returning to our King? For now is the time to wake from our sleep. Satan has blinded and bound us for far too long. It is time to leave our false delusions of what we previously believed and follow the truths of Scripture. For what would this world look like if we were to repent and awaken from our slumber? Could we even imagine it?

Imagine a people that actually lived out their lives following Christ. Imagine a land full of deep love and care, full of the Spirit. Imagine a people group who sought one another in all earnestness and desire, not out of obligation, sharing and giving in fullness. Imagine a people who, in kindness, gentleness, and self-control, refused to do spiritual harm to each other.

Imagine what it would be like if we were slow to speak and quick to listen, humble, and filled with joy. A group that cared more about the Lord than about our own egos. A people that only sought truth and righteousness, that quickly rooted out all evil for the sake of ourselves and our brethren, who refused to be shackled by selfish gain. Imagine being unashamed of our love for the Lord and truly representing the word "family."

For this image is not a dream. It is not only guaranteed in the future to come but also possible even now. Even in our mortal bodies, we can learn to live out this life as a people group filled with the Holy Spirit. In the past, it was described in Acts 2. The early church behaved like this during an extreme time in history. In that time period, persecutions and trials ran amok. Yet they were still a shining beacon of God's love, even then.

Likewise, do we not desire this to be true among our own people group? As believers, we are supposed to be living out our lives under our Lord. For we can still strive to be like Christ, even when it may seem pointless or impossible.

Let us begin by rooting out the evil within ourselves and the church body. Let us not be consumed with addictions, filled with lustful desires, or turn brother against brother. Instead, let us focus our attention back on God and think of what we *should* do rather than what we *can* do. Let us not remain as hypocrites.

For we should continue on the path after perfection, though we know it to be unattainable in this world. We should seek after God, our one and true love. Do not let the lies of Satan deceive us into believing all is lost. For the war has already been won. Who then shall we fear when the Victor already resides within us?

What other excuses, then, do we have left? Is it more knowledge that we require to follow Jesus? Do we need more time? Will we remain in despair with our continued justifications? Or are we finally ready to decide that it is time?

Because with God by our side, it is now our moment to be the example we so desperately crave. It is now time for us to get up and join in the spiritual battle against Satan and his legions. Let us take a stand with our fellow brothers and sisters in arms. Let us raise our flags to the King of kings while steeling ourselves in the face of adversity. For we have been handed all the equipment needed for battle.

And there are people who remain lost, waiting to be resuscitated and brought back to life. The sick and wounded are screaming for help! Who can arise to the challenge, except us who have been healed? It is through God our moment has now arrived. For we have been given the medicine and the good news! The only step remaining is to go! Only the call of destiny awaits—the call to challenge all of our presumptions and forfeit the very freedoms that we hold most dear. For the moment is quickly fading, and it is now our time to step forward.

www.ingramcontent.com/pod-product-compliance
Lightning Source LLC
Chambersburg PA
CBHW070851050426
42453CB00012B/2129

The Evolving Woman 21 Day

Start Living - Quit Apologizing

Duquesa D. Dean

Copyright @ 2020 by Duquesa D Dean.
All rights reserved. In accordance with the US Copyright Act of 1976, the scanning, uploading, and electronic sharing of any part of this book without the permission of the publisher is unlawful piracy and theft of the author's intellectual property. If you would like to use material from the book, (other than for review purposes) prior written permission must be obtained by contacting the publisher at duquesa@duquesadean.com.
Thank you for your support of the author's rights.

Visit the author's website at www.duquesadean.com

Duquesa is a Transformation & Motivational Speaker.

To book Duquesa, email duquesa@duquesadean.com

ISBN: 978-0-578-75743-8

About the Author

My life is multifaceted.

As a result of my Customer Service, Leadership, Branding & Strategy Training Sessions, businesses experience an increase in employee productivity as well as profits. They also benefit from a more engaged workforce.

Additionally, my web-based TV show Empowering Queens TV, supports & encourages women to pursue their dreams, to overcome limitations and to shatter boundaries.

As an author, my books focus on helping women develop the skills needed to reclaim their power and to rebuild their lives. My most recent book Sister Stand Up Again is a tool women have used to create a blueprint that to rebuild their lives.

I vividly remember sitting on my bathroom floor at the age of 30 considering tapping out on life. Up to that point in my life, I had basically been existing on auto pilot. My personal brand was truly lacking, and my goals were shallow. Those were the reasons I'd made poor decisions that made me feel hopeless.

With the help of a mentor, I rebuilt my life focusing on re-building my personal brand, becoming more educated and developing a better network of people to "play" with.

Fast forward to today, I'm using the lessons from those broken experiences to work with professional and business women, creatives and other women who are tired of being "stuck" and who are seeking personal or professional development.

As a result of the work I do with women they:

1. Experience a greater sense of purpose
2. Create and execute action plans
3. Live with less limits
4. Experience true joy.

I have invested deeply in my own development. Using the strategies and tools I learned from my various certifications and coaching, I help women unleash their full potential, overcome fear and be courageous enough to pursue their goals.

Dedication

I dedicate this book to my beautiful daughter Amber.

She has been by my side through the madness I call life. She sat in the background and watched as her mom shared herself with the world.

Not one who is interested in being in the spotlight, she has silently supported every effort, every dream, and every goal.

She is one of the sweetest people on earth, with a beautiful smile and a kind heart. She is one of the reasons, I stay in on this journey. She believes in me and often tells her friends her mom is nice.

There is much I desire for her. Happiness. Prosperity. Love. Very little pain. Joy. It is for this reason that I declare over her life and cover her future with spoken words that affirm just that.

"Sweet Thing", thank you for giving me a reason to live in my darkest hours. I love you more than words can express. Thank you for always being there and for loving me, in the good times, the bad times and in the hard times. Thanks for believing in me.

Love Always,

Mommy

Table of Contents

Day One - Acceptance of Your Truth 12

Day Two – Being Aware 18

Day Three - Making Choices 24

Day 4 - Facing Fears 30

Day 5 - Affirming Yourself 36

Day 6 - Being Courageous 43

Day 7 - Forgiveness 50

Day 8 - Loneliness 58

Day 9 - Letting Go 65

Day 10 - Purpose 74

Day 11 - Reflections 81

Day 12 - Inner Circle 87

Day 13 - Trust 94

Day 14 - Self-Love 100

Day 15 - Gratitude 108

Day 16 - Faith 116

Day 17 - Love 124

Day 18 - Failure 135

Day 19 - Beliefs 141

Day 20 -Seeing Your Value 149

Day 21 - Intentional Action 157

Other Valuable Resources 169

Credits: 170

The Daily Process

This twenty-one-day journey will require dedication and commitment to inner healing.

To move forward, to overcome challenges and to move past limitations, it is necessary to work to embark on a journey of personal development.

It is necessary to move past limiting self-beliefs and to improve self-esteem and self-image.

As a result of our life experiences, we may feel like we are not worthy of our dreams, but we are!

We must work diligently to reframe our thoughts.

Every day, over the next twenty-one days, at the end of daily exercises, there are affirmations to repeat. Affirmations help us to reframe our thoughts. To remove negative self-chatter we must replace it with more positivity.

Together, we will identify lies that we have been telling ourselves. Not only will we identify those lies, we will replace them with the truth.

This process will take WORK. There is no shortcut to healing.

It will be necessary to face your hurt and to be vulnerable enough to bare your soul to yourself with a view to identifying your triggers.

If at any point during the 21 days, it feels overwhelming, take smaller steps. The journey can be converted to a 21-week journey instead of twenty-one days by completing one lesson a week. This is your journey. Customize it for your pace.

It is my recommendation that you read the journal every morning before starting your day.

Create a safe space for yourself. You may also play soft instrumental music to set the atmosphere.

Before beginning the devotional, take a few minutes to meditate. Inhale deeply through the nose, hold for a few seconds and then exhale through your mouth. Repeat a few times.

Reserve at least 20 minutes per day to read and reflect on the day's lesson.

At the end of each lesson, write down your thoughts and understanding of the message. Identify your greatest takeaways and what opportunities exist for development are. Complete the daily affirmation to power you for the day ahead.

At the end of each day, complete the reflection exercises. Think about your day and make note of how you were able to implement the lessons. Identify what was easy and what was more difficult to complete.

The journey takes us into the core of who we are. If you encounter setbacks along the way, dust yourself off and start again. Trust & believe that you have the strength and fortitude to complete the process.

You are valuable gift to the world. God has a purpose for your life. Have faith that you can and you will achieve that purpose.

Faith without action is dead. This twenty-one-day journey is a great step in the right direction

Begin the process of releasing your shackles and watch God work in and through you.

Day One - Acceptance of Your Truth

I still thank God each time I think about how close I came to taking my life that Saturday afternoon seventeen years ago.

Looking at my life today, it is sometimes surreal that, that bruised and broken woman of the past, is living a life of purpose, happy and fulfilled.

If someone had told me back then that I would be living the life I am today, I would have laughed at them.

In the hardest moments of our lives, we look at our lives and only see the bad parts.

We focus on the poor decisions, the failure, and the disappointment.

Doing this makes it hard to see the good parts of our lives and can leave us sitting in victimhood.

Have you ever been there; been to a place where you were just hopeless?

That is where I found myself seventeen years ago.

Back then, on the day that I sat on the bathroom floor contemplating whether or not to take my life, I realized that while the various experiences that drove me to consider taking my own life were real, I had not really accepted responsibility for helping to create them.

When we do not take time to process and work through the experiences that damage us, we move from one experience to the next, tucking away the hurt, pain, shame, and disappointment we feel.

That is exactly what I had done and, as a result, the truth as I knew it was skewed by my negative experiences.

My inability to trust people was deeply rooted in the fact that most people, who should have protected me, abused me. This made me feel unworthy as well as suspect of true love.

I took a victim attitude towards life. Some of my thoughts were that people just did not like me. They did not value me. People do not stay in your life for long. They come and either they die or abandon you leaving you to struggle on your own.

These thoughts stemmed from an incredibly low self-esteem. The truth is I had created some of those lies to support my decision to keep people at arm's length.

Yes, I had some horrible experiences, but I also had some wonderful experiences.

I chose to hold on to the negativity to support my bad habits and bad choices.

The truth is I did not honor or respect myself.

We must search ourselves for the truth.

When we are bold enough to inspect ourselves, look at the root of our decisions and actions and really understand what is driving us, then and only then, we can make better decisions.

Essentially, the truth is what will set us free.

The truth is we already have everything we need inside of us.

When I finally accepted that it would be through my pain, that I would find my purpose, I found the courage to peel back the layers of hurt to heal them.

I was only able to step into my destiny after I discovered the truth behind my actions.

I had to forgive myself for inviting so much trauma and negativity into my life. I had to forgive myself for acting like less of a person;

for believing that I was not worthy of living out my life's purpose.

I had to forgive myself for dumbing down instead of living in my brilliance.

Forgiving me helped to heal me.

Tips on how to forgive yourself:

1. **Accept that you did the best you could with the knowledge you had at that time.**

2. **Commit to yourself, that now that you know better, you will do better.**

3. **Review your choices to discover the root of them. Ask yourself, "Why am I making these choices?", and then answer yourself truthfully.**

4. **Renew your mind by converting the experience into a lesson. Then take the lesson and make the future better.**

5. **Apologize to those you have hurt and make amends with them.**

6. Write yourself an apology letter. Start with writing your name and then use the stem sentence, "I am sorry for".

7. **Release it and free yourself.**

After reading today's entry, I realize:

Today I want to focus and work on:

Today's affirmation:

I am enough. I was born to live a whole healthy and happy life.

I will not allow the emotional baggage of my past to continue to weigh me down.

Today I will make decide to be happy.

Today I realize that my experiences can make me or break me.

I choose to allow them to make me.

I will not be broken. I will no longer be ashamed of my past.

I forgive myself for holding onto my past negative experiences and for having a victim attitude.

I am brilliant. I am beautiful. I am amazing. I am an overcomer. I am a Queen.

Today's reflections:

When forgiving yourself, what were you most resistant to?

Of the items you were most resistant to, which can you work on?

Day Two – Being Aware

It is amazing how many gifted, talented, and powerful women there are in the world.

Another thing that amazes me is that we only see a tiny fraction of ourselves. Other women who associate with us see just how big we are playing in the world, but we minimize ourselves.

I have trained myself to look in the mirror and to celebrate the woman I am. I celebrate my small wins and remind myself that I am beautiful, worthy, and enough. When I do this exercise, I walk away feeling proud of myself and feel the power within me.

I have trained myself to look at those small wins and to congratulate myself for them after all, small wins lead to big accomplishments.

This process took time though. It was uncomfortable at first, but I stuck with it until it felt normal.

Years ago, a friend I respect, and love repeatedly told me I did not see myself; that I was gifted and had a servant's heart.

It was not the first time I had heard that.

When my mentor first approached me offering to help me on my personal growth journey, he told me that he had observed my work ethic and saw my potential which is why he offered to mentor me.

Well guess what? I certainly had not seen it! I was quite confused.

The reality is that people sought me out all the time to assist with various projects, volunteer my time, help them to complete tasks, assignments and so much more.

I was usually given a heavy workload at the places I was employed at due to my record of timely completion of assignments. I always did more work than was asked or expected.

We tend to downplay our skills. Let that sink in for just a minute.

We tend to overlook our strengths and instead focus on our weakness.

We can stay stuck in situations where we see no way out because we are so focused on the problem and not the gifts, we have that can solve it.

How has your inability to look at the silver lining caused you to stay stuck?

The truth is people can see the potential or the talent in us that we may not be aware of.

I remember a manager at one of the places I worked at, telling me how influential I was. She saw my ability to connect well with people and to influence their decisions. I however was never aware of this specific talent and quite frankly did not even understand its value at that time.

As I started to evolve into a better woman, I pondered some questions. Those questions included:

1. What were the things people saw in me that I did not see in myself?
2. Why had I not taken the opportunity to assess myself?
3. What were my strengths?
4. What were my weaknesses?
5. What was I passionate about?
6. What did I absolutely detest?

My self-awareness journey did not begin until I aligned with my mentor who asked me who I was and I was unable to clearly articulate a response.

The first step in my journey was being aware of who I was; looking at myself and understanding my gifts and talents.

Why had I not done that before? Why had I not valued myself enough to determine who I was or who I wanted to be?

As silly as it seems, I had no clue that I could create myself; that I could figure out the attributes and characteristics I wanted aligned with my brand and be that.

Being aware requires thoughtfulness and intentionality.

What are the things that life is trying to show you?

Look at the signs and signals and become more aware of how your perspective is hindering your success.

Being able to understand and become aware of why we do the things we do, helps us to become more grounded and make better decisions for our lives.

Tips on how to be self-aware:

1. **Meditate – take time to sit in silence and listen to your own thoughts.**

2. **Monitor your emotions and reactions.**

3. **Identify your strengths.**

4. Establish healthy boundaries.

After reading today's entry, I realize:

Today I want to focus and work on:

Today's affirmation:

Today I commit to knowing myself better; to being aware of who I am.

I commit to receiving the messages I need to help me better understand whom I am.

Today, I will be intentional about what makes me exceptional.

I will not be sensitive to the areas where I need my greatest improvements.

I know that I am not perfect, yet I understand that I can strive for perfection.

I will accept my imperfections and allow myself to just be.

I will be aware of how my actions impact others.

I will take full responsibility for who I am and strive to be a better me.

I will be self-aware because I understand it is the key to peace.

I am brilliant. I am beautiful. I am amazing. I am an overcomer. I am a Queen.

Today's reflections:

When being self-aware, what were you most resistant to?

Of the items you were most resistant to, which can you work on?

Day Three - Making Choices

Denis Waitley advises us that "There are two primary choices in life: to accept conditions as they exist or accept the responsibility for changing them."

In full transparency, I admit, that I have not always made decisions that were in my best interest.

There were times when I made decisions because I did not want to rock the boat with a family member or a lover.

There were times when I made decisions while working in the corporate world to appease a "boss" or a team member.

There were even times when I made decisions to avoid upsetting my kids.

We do that. We do our absolute best to make everyone around us happy which also means we make ourselves unhappy.

Have you ever done that?

That day, as I sat on the bathroom floor contemplating whether to take my life or not, I made perhaps the most important decision of my life.

I decided to live but not just live a random life but to live a much better life than the one I had previously been living.

That one decision had a ripple effect in my life.

It was after deciding to live that my mentor approached me.

It was after deciding to live that I poured more love, affirmation, and healing into my kids.

It was after I decided to live that I started to remember my dreams again. The dreams I had as an eight-year-old child, as I sat outside at night gazing into the sky, wishing on stars.

I felt excited about my future and began making choices that supported my desire to live a better quality of life.

Life is about choices. While we may not like the things that are happening in our lives, we have the power to make different choices for better outcomes.

When we make a conscious decision to live by default, we are giving up our right to live the whole and happy lives we are capable of living.

Making decisions that go against the grain are not easy.

Our mind screams at us and tries to frighten us because it is no longer functioning in the "norm".

Fear rises and tells us that we cannot overcome; that we are weak and unworthy of better or of more.

We must be courageous enough to stare fear in its face and speak back to it. Let it know that you are valuable, you are worthy, and you have what it takes to make your dreams reality.

When you make the right choices about your life, you are free. You feel like you have more power over the direction your life is headed because you do.

In any situation you find yourself in, understand that you have the power of choice.

You do not need to be a victim and allow things to happen to you.

You have the right to make decisions about what is best for your life and to establish boundaries to ensure others are not able to trample over you.

Be mindful that every choice has consequences.

What are the consequences you are prepared to live with?

Be intentional about the choices you make!

Some choices lead to life lessons but even these are unbelievably valuable.

Strive to always make thoughtful, clear, and focused choices.

Make the type of choices that honor who you are, what you want and where you want to go.

Tips on how to make choices:

1. **Think about all the consequences.**

2. **Identify your emotions.**

3. **Focus on the big picture.**

4. **Consider the personal biases involved.**

5. **Seek advice from trusted people**

6. **Weigh the pros and cons.**

7. **Do not be afraid to do what is best for you.**

After reading today's entry, I realize:

Today I want to focus and work on:

Today's affirmation:

Today I will make choices that honor who I am.

I will not live by default.

I will make choices to help to improve my life even when those choices are difficult.

I will be grounded in my decisions.

I choose to be healthy and wise.

I choose to be optimistic.

I choose to look at the cup as half full and not half empty.

I choose to honor the divinity in me.

I choose to honor beliefs that align with my vision of me and my life.

I choose to be unapologetically me.

I am brilliant. I am beautiful. I am amazing. I am an overcomer. I am a Queen.

Today's reflections:

When making choices, what were you most resistant to?

Of the items you were most resistant to, which can you work on?

Day 4 - Facing Fears

Today, I can confidently board a plane, sit and conversate with another passenger, read a book or depending on the length of the flight, take a nap.

It was not always this way though

I remember being deathly afraid of flying. Yes, getting on a plane at any time would cause horrible anxiety. What if this plane crashes? How do I know that this pilot is experienced? Will I make it safely but more importantly alive to my destination?

My fear was so bad that one day as I sat on the plane, I started sweating and had a difficult time managing my anxiety. The plane doors closed and started its taxi down the airport strip. I was afraid, nervous, and anxious!

I remember the panic! I started crying uncontrollably and asked to be let of the plane. The pilot had to return to the gate to allow me to deplane.

I know you are laughing at me. It is okay. I laugh every time I remember this story as well.

We all have fears. Fears that stem from our beliefs. Fears that are not rooted in facts but are false expectations appearing real.

Fears prevent us from doings things that we in fact want to do.

As you think about it, how has being afraid stopped you from pursuing your dreams?

One day I decided I would face my fear of flying. This fear was unfounded. After all every single flight I took arrived safely so where was this fear stemming from?

As I pondered the question. The answer quietly dropped in. When I am on an airplane, I was flying it and therefore not in control.

To confront this fear, I challenged myself to take flights consistently.

As I took my seat on each flight, I silently prayed and acknowledged that God was in control.

I read books. I chatted with the people seated next to me. I listened to music. I did all of this to help soothe me.

Soon I challenged myself to take naps. This was the ultimate test, but I did it and gradually my fears dissipated.

The greatest fear I struggled with as a young mom was not being able to provide for my children after leaving my ex-husband. He was an excellent provider.

When I made the decision that I no longer wanted to live in fear of my life, I had to face an even greater fear. Would I be able to handle the responsibilities of being a working mother of two?

The enemy has a way of placing self-doubt in our minds when we make decisions that are best for us but are outside of our familiar zone.

Even though I was afraid to leave my marriage, I found the courage to do so.

One tool that really helped me to overcome some of my fears was to write them down, inspect them to see if there was any truth to it.

Writing them out helped me to identify the lies I told myself and then gave me the opportunity to correct the lie with the truth.

In the instance of leaving my marriage, I spoke to my fears. I acknowledged that I would be a good provider and a nurturer to my kids.

Within a year of leaving my ex-husband, I purchased my first home. I was so proud of this accomplishment and I was happy that I did not listen to my fears and instead conquered them!

I had to face my fears to move past them. I found out that at the root of fear lies doubt.

The more I believed in myself and in my ability to create a better life, the more willing I was to confront my fears and overcome them.

Tip to help when facing fears:

1. **Identity to root of the fear.**

2. **Chose positive thoughts when facing fears.**

3. **Visualize yourself overcoming your fear.**

4. **Plan then act. Having a plan of action provides a guide.**

5. **Journal your fears then under it write out the truth.**

6. **Practice gratitude daily.**

7. **Use affirmations to affirm yourself.**

After reading today's entry, I realize:

Today I want to focus and work on:

Today's affirmation:

God's plans for me are greater than man's plans for me.

"For I know the plans I have for you declared the Lord. Plans to prosper you and not to harm you. Plans to give you hope and a future." This is God's promise in Jeremiah 29:11.

I am confident in God's plan for my life.

I will not be afraid because I know He already knows the outcome.

I will not be anxious or worried.

Every day I will bravely face my fears with a view of overcoming them.

I release the need to be in control.

I acknowledge that fear can fuel me, and I will use it to do just that.

When I am afraid, I will be calm and confident.

I am fierce. I am brilliant. I am beautiful. I am amazing. I am an overcomer. I am a Queen.

Today's reflections:

When you were afraid, what were you most resistant to?

Of the items you were most resistant to, which can you work on?

Day 5 - Affirming Yourself

My mentor was adamant about daily affirmations.

As a young adult with a fragile self-esteem who was mentally battling so many negative experiences, he knew I needed to reframe my past to boost my confidence.

Every single day we repeated affirmations to focus on self-worth, self-value, overcoming challenges, embracing my gifts, and recognizing the divinity in me.

A few weeks of repeating the affirmations daily resulted in me believing in them. The power of the spoken word cannot be overstated.

I was listening to me describing myself, me as a chosen child of God, purpose driven, a confident woman, an overcomer, a high achiever with limitless potential and abilities.

I became a more confident person as a result. I believed in me.

Once I started believing in me, I was able to see myself more clearly. My self-confidence was boosted, and I believed that anything I put my mind to, I could achieve.

This mind shift also resulted in a better, improved version of me.

At work my performance increased which resulted in more opportunities, more promotions, and my career took off.

As I continued to affirm myself, I found less need for validation from others. I had taken the time to define the person I thought I was.

The power is doing this is that when we affirm ourselves, we benefit from more emotional stability. The need for external stability keeps us unstable. When we do not receive it, we spiral.

Once I had perfected affirming myself, and got a better sense of who I was at that time, I then wrote out a clear picture of who I wanted to be and set about living up to my vision for myself.

We are more powerful than we realize. We have the power inside of us to achieve our goals, dreams and to overcome our limitations. We have the power to change the trajectory of our lives. All of that power is within us!

Have you believed that who you are is not enough to do the things you really want to do or are called to do?

You have the power!

It takes work to rediscover ourselves and our power.

One of the ways we do this is by affirming ourselves.

To this day, I still repeat my affirmations. I feel powerful and unstoppable once I am done.

During my most emotional times, I find it necessary to remind myself of who I am, whose I am, and what my purpose in life is.

You see the enemy knows me well and understands that to derail me he must put me in an emotional crisis.

I had to counteract his plan and so I created affirmations specifically to heal my wounds when the enemy tried to open them or inflict more pain.

I wish I understood the power of affirmations earlier in life or that as a child I had been taught how to affirm myself. I imagine my life's journey would have been so much different if I had.

However, that was not God's plan for my life and I now realize that for my purpose to be fulfilled I needed to have the experiences I did.

I encourage you to make daily affirmations a part of your routine. By searching the internet, you can find affirmations for any need. As you become more familiar with yourself you can create your own affirmations.

I do not know about you, but I've heard time and time again about the power of the tongue.

Use it to speak life into yourself and to respond to the negative thoughts that lead to self-doubt, low self-esteem, and low self-value.

Tips on affirming yourself:

1. **Find a quiet space where you can look in a mirror.**

2. **Take a few deep breaths, in through the nose, hold for a few seconds and then release through the mouth.**

3. **Start with the words I am.**

4. **Make the affirmations specific to your needs.**

5. **Keep it brief and positive.**

6. **Affirm yourself daily.**

After reading today's entry, I realize:

Today I want to focus and work on:

Today's affirmation:

I love myself.

I am valuable.

I am worthy.

I am enough.

I am deserving.

I am more than the experiences of life that were designed to break me.

I believe in my talents and abilities.

I know that I was created to be the head and not the tail.

I am confident.

I honor the parts of me that need to improve. I will not belittle them.

I will focus my efforts on being the best me I can possibly be.

I will trust myself to make decisions that are best for me.

I will not allow the negativity of others to take away my joys.

The opinion of me that others have is just that, their opinion.

I know who I am, and I am confident in whom I am.

I am smart.

I am focused.

I will not play small.

I will embrace all that I am.

I am fierce. I am brilliant. I am beautiful. I am amazing. I am an overcomer. I am a Queen.

Today's reflections:

When being self-aware, what were you most resistant to?

Of the items you were most resistant to, which can you work on?

Day 6 - Being Courageous

My two favorite definitions of courage are "the ability to do something that frightens you; bravery" and the other is "strength in the face of pain or grief."

There is no healing or reframing without courage.

That night, the one where my ex-husband locked us in the house, it took all of my courage to leave.

I considered the consequences and decided in that moment that I needed to be brave and to do what was best for my children.

In the face of fear, uncertainty about the future as well as fear of not getting us out of the house before he returned, I worked as fast as possible to remove the bottom windowpane to provide an escape for us.

I was afraid. As I pondered what to do, I started thinking about who would provide for us if I left. How would we get around? I had no transportation of my own and both children would need to get to school. Where would I find lunch for them each day? What if they got ill and needed to see a doctor? Where would the money come from? How would their school fees get paid? Where would we live? Would my children be comfortable in the new environment? They were used to sleeping in their own beds.

I started to think about whether I had the strength to leave the marriage for good.

Women are taught that a relationship validates them. I had emotional issues and had been manipulated for a number of years so I started to think about whether I would ever be in another relationship again after all I had two young children; this would certainly be a burden that no man would want to deal with. I did not consider myself attractive or skilled. How would we ever make it?

What happened when you stayed in a situation that was toxic because you were too afraid to come out of your comfort zone?

We start to cycle negative thoughts in our minds and to focus on what could go wrong as we consider making decisions that are best for us.

This happens because we are afraid of change even when it is for the best.

We are creatures of habit.

That is how I felt that night as I worked feverishly to free me and my children.

Then I heard the words "do it afraid" in my head. Do it afraid? What did that mean?

I took it literally and increased my efforts to remove the windowpane, gently lowered my daughter, then my son to the ground all while assuring them everything would be okay.

My son was all for the adventure, he was too young to understand the danger, but my daughter was afraid.

After they were both outside, I started to work my way out of the window, while talking to them, assuring them that we would be okay.

My heart was pounding so hard in my chest. I was sure it would burst. My pulse was racing, and I was sweating.

In my haste to get out, I took nothing with us except the clothes we were wearing.

I felt broken and afraid, but I knew we had to get away. I was doing something that frightened me, but I needed to be strong. I needed to face my fears. I needed to be brave.

In that situation, I needed courage to overcome my self-doubt and to take action to get out of what was a really bad situation.

Many times, we stay in relationships, on jobs, and in situations that are harmful to us because we are afraid of the unknown.

Life has a way of providing exactly what you need when you are courageous enough to take the steps you need to give yourself a better life.

After retreating to our family abode, I made a firm decision that I would not return to our marital home. In retrospect, none of us were ready for the responsibilities of marriage.

When we are bold enough to recognize fear and confront it, we reclaim our power and take control of our lives.

Sis, believe that you are fearfully and wonderfully made by the Creator who loves you and who powers you.

You were created to have dominion and not to be dominated.

You were created to enjoy life while balancing good and bad.

Sometimes as women we do not believe we deserve all the happiness and joys that life can bring.

If you find yourself in an unhappy situation understand that you have the courage it takes to get out of it.

Have faith in yourself and in your ability to create the life you deserve.

Tips on being courageous:

1. *Acknowledge and embrace your fears.*

2. *Start by making small changes.*

3. *Celebrate small wins.*

4. *Find a buddy to support you.*

5. *Rediscover your self-esteem.*

6. *Practice positive self-talk.*

7. *Trust your gut instinct.*

8. *Visualize your ideal future.*

After reading today's entry, I realize:

Today I want to focus and work on:

Today's affirmation:

I am brave.

I am courageous.

My fears will not control me.

I will face them and overcome them.

I have an unlimited source of strength within me.

I will act despite my fears.

I am a warrior, daring and passionate.

I am fearless.

My challenges will not get the best of me.

I will face life's challenges with my head lifted high.

I will win my battles and if in the event I lose any, I will take the lessons to make me stronger the next time I face that situation.

I am fierce. I am brilliant. I am beautiful. I am amazing. I am an overcomer. I am a Queen.

Today's reflections:

When being courageous today, what were you most resistant to?

Of the items you were most resistant to, which can you work on?

Day 7 - Forgiveness

As a young woman, I had a lot of resentment in my heart toward the people in my life who I believed did not protect and nurture me appropriately.

I struggled through life with big chips on my shoulders.

I was hurt and angry.

In particular, I had a lot of anger towards my parents. I was upset with my father because he was not there for me when I most needed him.

The absence of a father in part was the catalyst behind my desire for male affection and love.

I was upset with my mom because after "Mother" who was my great-grand mother and primary nurturer died, I thought that she should have been there to help me through the difficult time.

I held onto those negative feelings and emotions for quite some time.

Anyone who had hurt me, neglected me, or ignored me, I resented and gave them plenty of attitude.

As I started working with my mentor, and shared my stories with him, he made it clear to me that I needed to heal those emotions to move forward in life. I needed to forgive those people to close what was obviously a gaping wound.

I thought my mentor had lost his mind! I strongly resisted this assignment.

These people had hurt me deeply and I was supposed to forgive them? Oh no! They needed to apologize to me and to reach out to make amends with me. This was my huge but fragile ego speaking.

We believe we are protecting ourselves when we hold on to bitterness and anger. We are hurting ourselves though.

The people we are holding resentment toward have moved on with their lives while we are still holding on and festering about the situation.

We tend to avoid processing our emotions and feelings.

For some reason, we have been taught to dump them in the emotional vacuum inside of us, to put on our big girl panties, to deal with it and to move on.

Somehow that is supposed to demonstrate that we are okay with whatever has happened because we cannot let people see how they impacted us.

How much better would your life be if you released the trauma, hurt & disappointment that keeps you angry?

My mentor pressed me to have conversations with the people who I needed to forgive just to hear their version of events and he reminded me that forgiveness was for my benefit - not theirs.

Well……………… eventually, I had those conversations.

As a result of them, I understood that my parents and other family members had lots going on in their lives and there were circumstances that prevented them from doing more to nurture me and in some instances, they loved at what was their full capacity.

As I listened to my mom tell her story, I was moved to compassion as I heard the troubles and trials, she endured through her pregnancy with me and during my early childhood.

I understood then why "Mother" who was my great-grandmother, was my nurturer and protector.

I was able to see that my mom allowed her to be my primary caregiver because she believed it was best for me at that time.

My dad had his own issues. Sometimes I got conflicting information, but I decided that forgiveness was more important as it would open the door to build a better relationship with him.

After I forgave them, I was able to release the pains, hurts and frustrations.

I felt a burden lifted.

I got answers that I needed but not all of the answers were easy to hear nor were all of them acceptable.

Nevertheless, I felt so much lighter.

The burden of carrying resentment was released and the emotional walls I had erected towards my parents started to come down.

The lessons I took from my conversations with my mom and dad were simple but profound.

Parents are people. All people have emotions, struggles and situations they are trying to balance. They are subject to weakness and can also become overwhelmed by life.

This lesson spills into my life every day now as I realize every single person I meet is struggling with something.

With this lesson, I now avoid judging people and give my best effort to forgive others when they are brash, rude, unthoughtful, etc.

I choose to forgive others because I understand their actions are not a reflection of me but instead a reflection of them.

Tips for forgiving self and others:

1. **Extend grace to yourself and others. Remember, everyone makes mistakes.**

2. **Acknowledge your emotions and don't get stuck in them. Feel them, then process them.**

3. **Take responsibility for the part you played in the situation.**

4. Express yourself clearly without attacking others. If necessary, wait until you are calm.

5. Take the lesson from the experience to avoid making the same mistake in the future.

6. Let it go. Do not hold onto hate, resentment, or anger.

After reading today's entry, I realize:

Today I want to focus and work on:

Today's affirmation:

I forgive those who have hurt me in the past.

Forgiving them does not make what they did right; it allows me to release the poison building in me as a result of holding on to hate.

I release the weight of the burden of resentment, hate and anger.

I forgive myself for holding grudges against others.

I forgive myself so that other others whom I may have hurt may also forgive me.

I forgive myself for believing that I deserved to feel the pain and bitterness I held on to because of not forgiving.

I release the hurt that have held me bound; that have prevented me from chasing my dreams and that have made me feel like less.

I let go of the past and look forward to a better future.

I am fierce. I am brilliant. I am beautiful. I am amazing. I am an overcomer. I am a Queen.

Today's reflections:

When forgiving others, what were you most resistant to?

Of the items you were most resistant to, which can you work on?

Day 8 - Loneliness

Avoidance is a serious thing! As a result of not wanting to face my issues and heal my hurt, I made sure that I spent as little time alone as possible.

I was always in the company of friends or family because being alone would provide space for my mind to think.

Even though I was often surrounded by others, I still felt a sense of loneliness.

There was this emptiness inside of me that felt like an endless empty hole.

I did not feel like I belonged anywhere.

I put on a brave face, smiled, and interacted in a personable way. To the people looking at me it seemed like I had it all together but honestly, I was crumbling inside.

Many nights after the company was gone, I would find myself staring into the ceiling with this longing; a longing to feel loved, wanted and appreciated.

I felt so alone and figured no one would understand my struggle. I felt empty inside.

The only emotion I could muster was the love for my children, nothing else really mattered.

This sense of emptiness and loneliness made me feel so hollow inside.

This sense of emptiness also drives us to fill it. We fill it by going from relationship to relationship.

We stay connected to people we should release for far too long to avoid being alone and facing ourselves.

I remember one day shortly after the end of a love relationship; I was out supporting a friend at a walkathon she had organized.

After the participants left the walk site, I was walking around the walk site waiting on their return when my friend approached me. She spoke to me and I did not realize she was able to feel my turmoil. She told me I looked empty and lonely. I was.

I felt lost; like I was in a wilderness. I felt like who I was, was not good enough unless I was attached to some love connection.

That was then though. Today, I embrace solitude and quiet time. I embrace and look forward to the moments when I have myself totally to myself.

We do our best to mask, hide and avoid dealing with ourselves. We avoid facing things that make us uncomfortable.

We stay in busyness to occupy our minds and to avoid the silence that allows us to think about the things that hurt our souls.

Have you been there?

It is not an easy place to be..... hurting and hiding it from ourselves.

It was not until I took the difficult journey to work through my pain that I was able to sit alone in silence.

After addressing the emotions that kept me handicapped, I wanted to spend time alone.

It was not until I had my breakthrough, the one that occurred after I rebuilt my life after contemplating suicide, that I understood I may have been lonely, but I was never alone.

Today, I am intentional about alone time.

My schedule can sometimes be hectic and so every opportunity I can get to be alone, I grab.

Being alone allows me to take care of me; to listen to my heart, to meditate and be grounded, to tap into the source that fuels my dreams, to unwind and relax.

I have learned to enjoy my own company.

When you are feeling lonely, have you ever paused to think about the root cause?

When you feel lonely again take a few minutes to discover why.

Learn to love yourself and to love your own company.

Being alone allows you to build a relationship with someone you can never live without . . . you!

Get to know who you are.

Frame the person you would like to be.

Find exciting and interesting hobbies.

Travel.

Do anything but sit and wallow in self-pity.

Tips on dealing with loneliness:

1. Acknowledge your feelings.

2. *Journal what actions you take when you are lonely.*

3. *Create a list of activities you enjoy and can choose from when you feel lonely.*

4. *Schedule time alone and practice being with yourself.*

5. *Schedule time to nurture valuable relationships and connections.*

After reading today's entry, I realize:

Today I want to focus and work on:

Today's affirmation:

Today I choose to love and value myself.

I am a unique and gifted individual who was born to live a divine purpose.

I am never alone.

I am always in the company of someone who loves and respects me.

That person is me.

When I feel lonely, I will remember that I am a gift to the world.

I will take pleasure in quiet times.

I will be purposeful about carving out time for me to sit in solitude.

I will spend time understanding who I am and what I want.

I will fill my emptiness with purpose.

Today I embrace the love of those around me.

I will love, validate, and approve myself.

I am fierce. I am brilliant. I am beautiful. I am amazing. I am an overcomer. I am a Queen.

Today's reflections:

When feeling lonely, what were you most resistant to?

Of the items you were most resistant to, which can you work on?

Day 9 - Letting Go

Can I tell you one of the things I find most amazing in this life?

When our experience with a thing or a person is over, regardless of our resistance to it, the Creator ensures it ends.

Letting go of people and circumstances was once one of my weaknesses.

I would think about how difficult the road ahead would be or how much it would hurt the other person involved.

I thought of everyone and everything other than me.

Letting go is hard to do particularly when you have invested years of your life.

Let me tell you about John.

I thought John was the guy of my dreams.

At the time I met him, he was ending a tumultuous relationship with someone else or so he told me.

We began communicating daily and our communication increased to multiple times a day.

We eventually began dating and were soon in a relationship. At the point we entered a relationship, John was supposedly free and unattached.

John was thoughtful, personable and a gentleman. I looked forward to our Saturday outings.

Every Saturday was date night. We would go dancing, out to dinner and sometimes just holding hands while taking a walk.

He would open doors for me to enter establishments, open and close the car door, carry my handbag, buckle my shoes, massage my head while we watched television and so much more.

When we were not together, we would spend hours on the phone. Most nights we spoke for at least an hour prior to saying goodnight. In many instances, we spoke for two to three hours per night. Our conversations were about any and everything. It was a great connection.

As our relationship progressed, John's actions started to seem "shady".

As a process improvement professional, I have been trained to notice patterns and behaviors.

I watched these inconsistencies for a while.

As time passed and the patterns became more obvious, I spoke to John about my concerns.

He was adamant I was imagining things or reading too deeply into his actions.

It was at this point that I should have let go of John, but I did not.

It was hard facing the demise of another relationship particularly when we have been taught that we are defined by whether we are in a love relationship or not. I felt uncertain and anxious about rocking the boat.

We have a tendency of rationalizing red flags when we want a relationship so badly. We explain away bad behavior. We make excuses for actions that we should address. We avoid anything that would disrupt our fairytale beliefs.

What would your life be like right now if you had only accepted the red flags that clued you in to the fact that something was wrong in a situation?

Well, a few more months passed that were filled with inconsistent behavior and secrecy.

I decided that as much as I liked John, I needed to complete this relationship by letting him go.

No matter how many times I released him, John continued to call and to come, pleading his love and devotion.

For almost a year of my life, I engaged in this up and down relationship with John until finally one day in December I asked John to please leave me be as I was unsettled in our relationship and did not feel that I could trust him. John finally obliged.

Two weeks later I was sitting in the hair salon talking with my stylist.

We were discussing my recent break-up and how difficult it must have been on the heels of Christmas.

I shared some photos of us with my hair stylist. After looking at the pictures, my stylist sat in the middle of her shop floor saying no way. She looked at me and John was her first cousin's husband.

Imagine my disbelief. I was hurt deep to my soul because of this deception.

I told her there was no way this man was married. He spent so much time at my home. I could not get home soon enough after work for him to arrive. He would stay well into the night often.

Whenever he left, we would speak the entire time as he drove home and even after he had gotten home, we would still talk for a while.

It was impossible that this man was married.

I felt like a ton of bricks had hit me in the chest.

Have you ever been deceived so deeply?

It turns out that John was a great liar. He had lied to his wife and told her he was traveling for work on the nights he slept at my house.

He would speak to me from his home office at night.

John had a separate house from his marital home; one his father had willed to him when he died. This is where we spent time.

John's wife was distraught when she discovered his unfaithfulness, but she was also not surprised as her husband had done been unfaithful to her in the past.

I was devasted. The man of my dreams was a liar and fraud.

Why did I not let this relationship go when I first noticed those patterns?

My gut was telling me something was wrong so why was I so trusting of John's words?

Letting go of John equated to failure to me. It was another failed relationship. It was like being abandoned all over again. To avoid dealing with those emotions and feelings it was easier for me to stay with him than face that pain.

Letting go can be difficult.

It could be a love relationship, a family member, a friend, a job, a church, etc. If it is not making you happy, if it is causing you pain, if the situation is unhealthy for you . . . let it go.

After I was hit with the ton of bricks called John's deception, I garnered the support of my inner circle.

My closest friends rallied around me and in moments of weakness when the tears flowed, they would comfort me and remind me of who I was and whose I was.

Their support helped me through this difficult time.

I had let John go before and he always found his way back in.

The last time I released him the Creator made sure there was no back door in by exposing his other life.

Today, I am in a wonderful loving relationship with a man who honors and respects me. He encourages me to live to my fullest potential and to chase my dreams. He supports me and nurtures me. He loves me.

Although the situation with John hurt me deeply and letting go of him was painful, it was a necessary step for me to have the wonderful relationship I have today.

Tips for letting go:

1. **Recognize the red flags in any situation.**

2. **Assess your reluctance to let go. What is it rooted in?**

3. **See the situation for what it is and not what you want it to be.**

4. **Identify the lessons the experience taught you.**

5. **Devote & volunteer your time to something larger than yourself.**

6. Keep your mind on what you can control.

After reading today's entry, I realize:

Today I want to focus and work on:

Today's affirmation:

Today I will trust that all things work together for my good.

I forgive myself for holding on to negative emotions and baggage.

I forgive myself for holding on to people and situations much longer than I should have.

I accept my past as my past and will pay attention to my gut instincts and to the clues that life provide.

I know that I am strong because of everything I have been through.

I know that letting go does not mean I am losing but rather that I am making room for something better to come into my life.

I am fierce. I am brilliant. I am beautiful. I am amazing. I am an overcomer. I am a Queen.

Today's reflections:

When you are lonely, what are you most resistant to?

Of the items you were most resistant to, which can you work on?

Day 10 - Purpose

As I stood on the stage talking to the women in the audience at the conference, it hit me. It was all for a purpose!

The reason I had had all these of life experiences was so that I could help others know that they can overcome their circumstances and turn their lives around.

There is nothing like understanding the why behind the what!

There were many occasions I asked God why me and never got a response. Sometimes I felt abandoned and forgotten while I navigated those experiences.

Why did it have to be me to have so many painful life experiences?

Why were the first thirty years of my life so difficult?

The truth is "he who feels it knows it" and unless we have been in someone else's shoes we cannot properly relate to their experiences.

As I stood on that stage and shared my life experiences, I realized that God had a greater purpose for my experiences and a huge purpose for my life.

Living in purpose has allowed me to use the pain from my past to help hurting women and teens girls move past their pain/trauma of their past and as a result they go on to achieve their goals, create better lives and to surpass self-imposed limitations.

We hide our life lessons, afraid that people would judge us if they knew about them.

We are ashamed of the mistakes we made in life and do our absolute best to make sure no one knows about them.

What if the lessons from your mistake is the exact knowledge another woman needs to help her avoid and/or overcome that exact situation?

An abused woman who escaped with her children through a window in search of a better life can relate to another abused woman in ways a woman who has not been abused can.

A woman who has had painful and/or traumatic experiences in her teenage years, can connect better with another teen navigating rocky situations.

Every experience we have had in life has a purpose.

Each of us has a purpose to fulfill and these stores can help to inspire and motivate others.

Many women feel as if they are alone in their situations or that no one would understand if they shared them.

You are not alone. Your experience is not limited to you.

You can use your life experience purposefully to help others along the way.

Living a purpose driven life is so rewarding. Knowing that you have given a sister a boost, some hope, some steps to find her way gives you a sense of satisfaction.

Being able to relate to what other women are experiencing and then being able to share with them how you overcame your situation gives purpose to your pain.

I decided to step into my purpose a few years ago. I was afraid. I wondered if I could be so vulnerable by exposing my private struggles. I wondered if people would listen to and believe in me. I acted in spite of those fears.

My dream of helping young women and men rise above circumstances and chase their dreams, kept me up at night.

I had visions and dreams of the steps I should take to make my dream of inspiring others come true.

I also realized that my dream of helping others was not of me, but it was God's plan for me.

As I started living in purpose, doors opened, and opportunities arose. I felt so alive! I felt proud of myself. I felt courageous and purposeful.

We can make a huge difference in the world, if we choose to shine the light and be a beacon of hope for others.

I encourage you to embrace your purpose and live it out passionately.

Tips to live in purpose:

1. ***Live your personal beliefs and values.***

2. ***Create your vision statement.***

3. ***Identify your strengths and passions.***

4. Seek to serve others from your overflow.

5. Take care of yourself first to avoid burnout, resentment and becoming detached.

6. Establish your priorities.

7. Follow your heart.

8. Invest in your future.

9. Be resilient.

After reading today's entry, I realize:

Today I want to focus and work on:

Today's affirmation:

My life's purpose is greater than me.

I realize that every experience is a part of a much larger plan.

I realize that no one else can fulfill my purpose.

I embrace it and walk in it.

My presence on the earth will positively impact the lives of others.

I will find meaning in my life.

God made no mistake when He created me.

I am created to fulfill a purpose.

I will mediate and listen to my inner guide.

I can make a difference in the world.

I will focus on the things I can do.

I am on the correct path.

I embrace all that I am.

I am fierce. I am brilliant. I am beautiful. I am amazing. I am an overcomer. I am a Queen.

Today's reflections:

When being self-aware, what were you most resistant to?

Of the items you were most resistant to, which can you work on?

Day 11 - Reflections

I never realized the value of daily reflections until about two years ago.

I could have literally slapped myself for not appreciating the amount of growth that comes from reflecting on my experiences.

Now, every single day, I reflect on the activities of the day to see what went well, what opportunities for improvement exist and what best practices stood out.

Being able to review the past allowed me to put some things into perspective.

After aligning with my mentor, one of the more difficult assignments he gave me was to review my life experiences with a view of seeing what learning I could garner from each of them.

I thought this was an odd request after all hadn't all of those things happened to me? I was the victim here!

I had made a commitment however to allow my mentor to help me develop and grow and so I obediently began the assignment.

As I looked at each experience and thought about what lessons I learned from them, I was amazed that each one taught me multiple lessons; lessons that I had not paid attention to or acknowledged previously.

We allow such wisdom to slip through our fingers when we do not find the lessons in situations that hurt us.

We do a disservice to ourselves by not inspecting our choices and actions to determine how we could have shown up differently, which would have resulted in a better outcome.

When we can inspect our experiences, and grab the lessons, we can make better decisions when faced with the same or a similar situation.

How has reflecting on your experiences helped you to make better choices?

For example, when I reflected on how the teacher at the school I had attended tried to take advantage of my innocence, I understood that you cannot always take people at face value. Even the most distinguished person can have malicious intent so we cannot judge someone's intentions by the position they hold.

I also learned that my need for a father figure made me vulnerable to such attacks. As a result, I now take the time to really get to know people. In addition to listening to what they say, I observe behaviors over time to get a better understanding of how they relate to others and to me. People show us who they are. Our job is to see it and to accept it.

Each experience that I reflected on taught me a valuable lesson.

Even today, as I reflect on the events of a particular day, week or quarter, I do so with a view of learning from every experience in order for me to make better and wiser decisions the next time I am faced with a similar situation.

I also find that when I am successful, I learn what works and I use that information to continue to be successful in that area.

Reflecting on our life experiences and on our daily, weekly, or monthly action is a good way to create a better future.

The past can help to make the future better but only if we use the lessons to make us wiser, better, and stronger.

When we harness the power of the past, and not just our past, but learn from the experience of others, we avoid heartache, headaches and we become more successful in a more efficient way. This is the reason coaching and mentoring is vital.

Tips to use the power of reflection:

1. **Be open and honest with yourself.**

2. **Create your values and beliefs.**

3. **Question why you do the things you do. Look at the root cause of your actions. Journal your thoughts and actions to identify patterns**

4. **Look for the things you do well and celebrate them.**

5. **Repeat the actions that bring you success.**

6. **Identify the actions that create problems or setbacks and avoid those.**

After reading today's entry, I realize:

Today I want to focus and work on:

Today's affirmation:

I will learn from my experiences.

I declare that the lessons of my past will propel me into my brilliant future.

I will use my success as motivation to continue being successful.

When I fail, I will take the lessons from each failure to make my tomorrows better.

I will not be defeated by my losses because they provide me with valuable lessons.

I will embrace each lesson and do the work I need to do to free me from any bondage.

I am in control of my life and of my destiny.

I am fierce. I am brilliant. I am beautiful. I am amazing. I am an overcomer. I am a Queen.

Today's reflections:

When doing the reflection activities, what were you most resistant to?

Of the items you were most resistant to, which can you work on?

Day 12 - Inner Circle

As a young child, my grandmother used to tell me "birds of a feather flock together" but the full meaning of her statement did not hit me until my final year of high school.

It was the night after I had attended the birthday party that my Auntie Ria had dropped me.

I left that party with "friends" to attend another party which was more "fly" than the one we were at.

I had just started attending a new school and wanted to make new friends and to fit in so badly.

When the popular girls invited me to go with them to another party and promised we would be back before my pickup time, I did not hesitate.

I hopped into the car with them and off we went to the next party.

I had such a fun time. We laughed, danced, and joked around so much so that my pickup time passed without us even realizing it.

My new friends were my "flock" and I had allowed them to influence my decisions some of which were really poor.

Today I fully understand the value of having the right people in your inner circle.

It is said that we are the average of the five people we hang around with most. Well so my mentor said.

As our mentorship progressed, he required me to find a circle of friends who were just as interested in personal growth as I was.

He wanted me to begin associating with likeminded people as in his opinion, that type of association would keep me focused on the goal, help me to help others on the same journey and also allow them to help me to grow as well.

Our inner circle of friends should be the people encouraging us to become better versions of ourselves.

Our inner circle of friends consists of the people nearest to us and their influence rubs off on us consciously and unconsciously.

We must be extremely strategic in selecting them.

Our inner circle members should be as strong as we are or stronger. These are the people who will encourage us to continue chasing our dreams. These are people who will support us as we pursue our goals.

They will hold us accountable, cheer for us and correct us.

These are people as gifted or as talented as we are; people who will help us to continue to grow.

Our inner circle protects us. When we are vulnerable, they hold us up and speak into our lives.

We tend to choose friends and/or associates who are not as strong as us. It is a safe way, to avoid being challenged or so that we can show ourselves as the smartest person in our group.

When this happens, we rob ourselves of the opportunity to learn from others. We also rob ourselves from building networks that include people who are strong in our area of weakness.

We risk feeling inadequate when we compare ourselves to others who stronger and more successful than us. Comparison is said to be the thief of joy.

Were you ever threatened by someone you could learn from and therefore did not develop a friendship with them?

My mentor lived the values he taught me. His inner circle is filled with people who are just as influential as he is and who challenged him to stay on top of his game.

As I released some people in my life, I watched my transformation really begin.

As I started associating with more successful people, my desire to achieve their level of success increased.

I worked harder. I read more books and stayed abreast of current events. You just never knew what subject would come up and I wanted to be sure I could speak as competently as they did.

I was forced to stay on the cutting edge. This new circle helped to refocus me and helped me to transform my life. This resulted in me feeling stimulated and mentally alive.

Today my inner circle holds five people who are as progressive as I am. These are the people who help me to pursue my dreams relentlessly and who I push to live their best lives. We celebrate each other and help each other in times of need.

In this circle, I feel stimulated, accountable, and responsible for being the best version of myself possible. Each of the other inner circle members feel the same way.

Your circle of friends will influence you. Select them wisely.

How to select a good inner circle of friends?

Tips to build a good inner circle of friends:

1. ***Establish your vision, mission, and core values.***

2. ***Consistently live those values.***

3. ***Attract people with similar values.***

4. ***Choose people who will hold you accountable.***

5. ***Choose people who you have chemistry with.***

6. ***Give as much as you take from the relationship.***

7. Select people who have proven they are trustworthy.

8. Select people who are positive and optimistic about the future.

After reading today's entry, I realize:

Today I want to focus and work on:

Today's affirmation:

I am worthy of loving relationships.

I deserve friendships that are rich and rewarding.

I deserve friendships that are positive and uplifting.

I will be the kind of friend who encourages others to live their best lives.

I will hold my friends accountable and be open and honest with them.

I will set a good example of friendship for my inner circle.

I choose to have good hearted people in my life.

I will also release friendships when they go against my values and beliefs.

I am fierce. I am brilliant. I am beautiful. I am amazing. I am an overcomer. I am a Queen.

Today's reflections:

When being self-aware, what were you most resistant to?

Of the items you were most resistant to, which can you work on?

Day 13 - Trust

For most of my young life, I struggled with trust issues. After those responsible for nurturing me, like the schoolteacher, my stepfather, and the father of a friend at school, I had no trust of or respect for me.

My trust issues got worse after I was betrayed by someone I loved.

He was a thoughtful and hardworking young man. I was a young naïve girl. This was my first real relationship and trusting him was already difficult for more reasons than one.

Coupled with the fact that the men who had been responsible for my care had tried to take advantage of me and having a father who was absent during my young life, I struggled with feeling unloved, and as a result this made being in a relationship difficult.

The trust declined when a young lady who we will call Danae, started dating my boyfriend.

Now, I had no idea about this affair, but one of the young boys who hung around my then boyfriend told me. He said that I was too nice a girl and too pretty to have someone scheming on me. I asked my daughter's father if he was being unfaithful and he denied it.

I did not need anyone to tell me he was "stepping out". My gut had already told me something was off, but I did not trust my gut either.

We know deep inside of us when something is not right. We have this sixth sense that prompts us. The thing is, we do not always trust that prompt. We second guess ourselves.

What experience in your life would have been better if you had only listened to that prompt?

As you can imagine, being betrayed by the people I loved was extremely difficult and with each betrayal trust was harder and harder to give.

When I started working with my mentor, we discussed all the possibilities surrounding why I attracted these sorts of relationships.

I finally settled on this reason.

I wanted to reinforce my unworthiness to myself.

By choosing men who would dishonor me, I would be validating a belief I grew up with; that I was not worthy to be loved.

I was embarrassed to acknowledge this truth.

The reality is I had not dealt with my issues.

As a matter of fact, I did think that all men were alike. You could not trust them. My teacher, best friend's brother and stepfather had already demonstrated that all men were the same; not trustworthy and only seeking sex.

It was not until I had healed myself and dealt with all of the emotions that I had dumped into the never-ending hole in my soul that I began to have better relationships.

I started trusting myself more. When my gut spoke to me, I listened to what it said. All men are not alike and to have a better-quality relationship, I needed to make better choices regarding who I got involved with.

After I trusted myself to love and value me and to see things as they are and not how I wanted them to be, I was able to have better relationships with my friends, family and romantically.

I still work on trusting because at times ugly thoughts pop up.

When they do, I assess them. Where are they stemming from? What is the real cause? Is there any truth to the fear? Whatever the answer is, whatever the truth is, I accept.

Now I fully trust me to do what is best for me.

Tips on trust:

1. ***Peel back the layers of previous betrayal to discover the root cause.***

2. ***Build your self-confidence. Replace the negative self-talk with more positive chatter.***

3. ***Validate and affirm yourself daily.***

4. ***Identify red flags in any situation and accept them.***

5. ***Believe your intuition.***

6. ***Ask questions and listen to the answers.***

7. ***Take time to get to know others.***

8. ***Observe how others act. People show you who they are.***

9. ***Believe them when they show you.***

After reading today's entry, I realize:

Today I want to focus and work on:

Today's affirmation:

I trust the process of life.

Every experience I have had was designed for a purpose to be fulfilled.

I am worthy of trusting myself and so I will trust myself and will listen when my inner spirit speaks to me.

My inner self already knows what to do.

I will honor myself.

I know that God will take care of my needs so I will trust him.

I am worthy of loving relationships built on trust.

I will trust my own decisions.

I am fierce. I am brilliant. I am beautiful. I am amazing. I am an overcomer. I am a Queen.

Today's reflections:

When are you most resistant to when thinking about trusting others?

Of the items you were most resistant to, which can you work on?

Day 14 - Self-Love

I sat on the phone talking to the person I was romantically involved with.

It was one of those occasions when we were discussing the future of our relationship.

It was obvious that the relationship was not working but none of us wanted to take the painful step to release the other, so we continued these conversations and created plans on how to improve the relationship.

On this occasion of us discussing the way forward, we were talking about a compromise on his need for space and my need for time.

As the conversation progressed, he started to get angry.

The angrier he got the more he lashed out. The harder he lashed out, the smaller I felt myself getting.

I started backing off and my thoughts turned to how to soothe him and to just give up what I needed so that he could be happy.

As he lashed out at me, I started to think about how the argument was my fault. I was thinking about his needs and even though I knew that my need was not unreasonable, I was willing to put it aside, at least momentarily, to have the argument go away.

I did not want him to be so angry about it that I did not see him for a few days. When he got angry, he would usually steam for a few days before coming around which really defeated the purpose of the discussion.

When we are struggling with self-worth and self-esteem issues, we avoid conflict as best as possible. We give in to others and shrink our desires. We do our best to please other people even if it means sacrificing ourselves.

You have value! You deserve to be treated well. You deserve to be heard. You deserve honesty. You deserve respect.

What do you feel like when you give in to others just to keep the peace and avoid losing your loved one?

This relationship was filled with conversations about how to make things better. The conversations usually ended up in me giving up the thing I wanted so that I did not lose him or the relationship.

Considering all the experiences I had gone through and the fact that abandonment issues were a part of my baggage, it was easy to put the needs of someone else consistently above mine, just to be in a relationship even if that relationship did not bring me joy.

Why did I not love myself enough to walk away from this situation earlier than I did?

Why did I not love myself enough to stick to my guns about what my needs were?

Why was I willing to let my needs go when I knew that my needs were reasonable and, in some instances, deal breakers?

Why did I shrink as he got angry?

Why did I back pedal when I knew I should have calmly stated my position on what my needs were and let the chips fall where they may?

Did I care more about his comfort and his need to be soothed than I cared about my own needs?

Why was I so willing to disregard my own well-being and happiness in exchange for his?

Why did the love from someone else matter more than the love I had for myself?

These were extremely hard questions I had to ask myself. These were the questions that made me dive into the bottomless emotional tank I threw my feelings into hoping to avoid dealing with them.

The answer was clear. I did not love myself.

I did not love and value myself and what I contributed to the relationship.

As a matter of fact, I did not recognize that the demise of the relationship was a greater loss for him than it was for me.

That was then. Now, I am confident in who I am. I can express myself calmly. I can comfortably sit in conflict without questioning or diminishing my worth. Now, I am not afraid to lose people because I do not want to risk losing myself ever again.

Learning to love myself was a process.

Over time, I learned to appreciate my strengths and to accept my weaknesses.

I learned that I did not need to be liked and that some people would not like me for reasons that had nothing to do with me.

I learned to validate myself; to look in the mirror and embrace the beauty that stares back at me.

I completed my affirmations daily and set off on my daily journey with a positive outlook.

I spent time alone talking to and listening to myself.

I embraced new hobbies and found talents I did not know I possessed.

I took the time to identify what I needed from my relationships be it family, friend or romantic.

I took the time to figure out what was negotiable and non-negotiable. I took the time to fully embrace all that I am.

This changed the game for me. This released my shackles and freed me up from the bondage of needing external validation and acceptance.

You too hold the power, to discover who you are and to be courageous enough to develop into the best and highest version of yourself to life.

Free yourself.

Tips on loving yourself:

1. *Rest your mind, body, and soul. Allow yourself time to rejuvenate.*

2. *Extend grace to yourself for your past mistakes and failures*

3. *Affirm yourself daily.*

4. *Discover a new hobby or passion.*

5. *Eat healthy food that fuels your body.*

6. *Stand in the mirror and challenge yourself to find at least 10 things you love about yourself. Then tell yourself, these are the reasons, why you love you.*

7. *Speak positively to yourself.*

8. *Cultivate an attitude of gratitude. Find things to be thankful for every day.*

9. *Exercise at least thirty minutes per day for a minimum of five days a week.*

After reading today's entry, I realize:

Today I want to focus and work on:

Today's affirmation:

Today I chose to love me.

I fully embrace who I am.

I recognize that I am not a perfect being.

I know my strengths and understand my weaknesses.

There is so much about me to celebrate.

I will honor and celebrate me every day.

I will not tear myself down with negative thoughts or words.

I will honor myself by saying no when I need to and I will honor my feelings when they arise.

I make mistakes but I am not a mistake.

I am loved

and appreciated. I am confident in who I am.

I am strong and more powerful that I can even imagine.

I accept and love my physical flaws because they make up a part of me.

I am wanted.

I am resilient. I am fierce. I am brilliant. I am beautiful. I am amazing. I am an overcomer. I am a Queen.

Today's reflections:

What are you most resistant to when it comes to loving yourself?

Of the items you were most resistant to, which can you work on?

Day 15 - Gratitude

Melody Beattie explains best how I feel about gratitude.

She says that "Gratitude makes sense of our past, brings peace for today, and creates a vision for tomorrow."

As I started to reshape my life with the guidance of my mentor, there were so many experiences and people I was grateful for.

Another way my mentor helped me to heal was by asking me to think about my experiences and find at least three things in each of them I was grateful for.

At the beginning, it was not an easy task. These were negative experiences so why in the world would I find anything about them to be grateful for?

As I started this exercise, I really had to think deeply but as I moved from experience to experience the process became easier.

Here are some of the things I identified as I completed this assignment.

I was grateful for life and for the opportunity to be mentored by a successful executive.

I was grateful that I had not taken my life that dreadful day when I sat on my bathroom floor with a bottle of tablets and a jug of juice.

I was grateful that I had been able to leave a marriage that was destroying me mentally, physically, and psychologically – many women do not make it out alive.

I was grateful that I was able to face depression and win.

I was grateful for the support of my family and friends as I navigated the various stages of life.

I was grateful that my kids and I were able to escape through that opening in the window the night we fled our home in fear that our lives were in danger.

I was grateful that I had a home to run to; a place where a village of people helped me to recover from the abusive marriage.

I was grateful to have a safe place where my kids would be comfortable.

I was grateful that my children were able to heal from the trauma they witnessed and were able to bloom into two well rounded adults.

I was grateful that my grandmother reached out to Social Services Child Services Division for help me who was labeled a "troubled" teen.

I was grateful that Maria Kelley responded to my grandmother's plea and provided me with love, support, and a haven where I felt loved and safe.

I was grateful that my mom and I developed a wonderful relationship. I was grateful that I was able to be with her and nurse her through her fights with cancer.

I was grateful for the wisdom and guidance I found in my father. He helped me to navigate many life issues successfully and I was grateful that I was able to forgive and to let go of the past.

I was grateful that Ms. Culmer, my eighth-grade teacher, saw my potential and inspired me to study and to write short stories.

I am grateful for having had thirteen wonderful years with my great grandmother.

I was grateful for the relationships that had not worked out; they taught me what I did not want.

I was grateful that I had to go to church every Sunday, Wednesday, and Friday. It was at church that I learned about God's grace and love.

That surely is a lot of gratitude isn't it?

We have this tendency of focusing on the negative without acknowledging the positive in hard situations.

We get so caught up in the bad parts of the experiences that we fail to find the gifts wrapped in sandpaper.

These gifts or life lessons provide valuable insights we can use to make the future better.

If you inspect your hard experiences, what lessons do you think you find?

I am grateful for each experience I have had thus far in life. They have all prepared me to step into my purpose and into my destiny.

I am grateful and humble that God chose me to help broken women, men, boys and girls breakthrough the limitations that hold them back.

I am grateful that I am a living testimony that you can overcome the past and create a better future.

Reframing my thoughts and experiences allowed me to take the lessons I needed from each and leave the rest behind.

As I reframed my mind, I began to embrace each day with a sense of gratefulness and humbleness. This allows me to be happy and to look forward to the future with hope and anticipation.

I agree with William Arthur Ward; "Gratitude can transform common days into thanksgivings, turn routine jobs into joy, and change ordinary opportunities into blessings."

Even in the most challenging circumstances, I look for the silver lining and find a way to be grateful for it.

Tips on cultivating an attitude of gratitude:

1. ***Keep a gratitude journal. List daily the things you are grateful for.***

2. ***Search for the silver lining in each experience.***

3. ***Thank people daily.***

4. ***Do not compare yourself to other people.***

5. Give back by sharing your talents, resources, or time with others. Volunteer to assist your church or community.

After reading today's entry, I realize:

Today I want to focus and work on:

Today's affirmation:

I have so much to be thankful for.

I am grateful to God for life and for all the blessings I experience.

I am grateful for family and friends.

I attract good things into my life because I am grateful.

I am grateful for the blessings that are on their way.

I am grateful for the small pleasures in life.

I am grateful that I am enough.

I am grateful for grace.

I am grateful for the love I receive every day.

I am fierce. I am brilliant. I am beautiful. I am amazing. I am an overcomer. I am a Queen.

Today's reflections:

What are you most resistant to when it comes to cultivating an attitude of gratitude?

Of the items you were most resistant to, which can you work on?

Day 16 - Faith

As my mom struggled to recover from her first battle with cancer, I stood at her bedside praying that God would provide her the strength and the desire to fight and to live.

After her surgery, she lay in bed painful but alive.

This was another one of those gratitude moments. I was grateful that she had successfully pulled through the surgery.

Having spent quite a lot of my teen years in church, I knew how to pray.

As I visited with her two to three times per day, I prayed that God would heal her body and heal her mind.

I can only imagine the amount of emotional turmoil a breast cancer survivor experiences when they first lose a breast and so I prayed, and I prayed.

I had faith that God allowed my mom to have this experience for a reason and trusted Him to give it purpose.

Apart from praying, I gave strict instructions to everyone visiting. My mom would beat this disease and she would live to tell the tale. I had faith that God would heal her body, heart, and spirit and no one and I meant no one would be allowed to speak anything but positive words of encouragement.

They were to speak life and to inspire her to give her best effort to recovering.

Everyone would express faith in her ability to fight and in God's ability to heal.

Anyone expressing negativity would be asked to leave her hospital room.

This was a strong stand to take. I agree. It was quite a necessary one to protect the energy in her recovery room.

During the time my mom spent in hospital, I prayed with more fervor. I believed without a shadow of a doubt that God would heal her.

When I entered her hospital room each morning, I prayed a blessing over her, the room, her doctors, and nurses as well as anyone who would be visiting that day.

Every evening I left, I prayed for her and for her healing. I had faith that she would emerge stronger than she was before.

I also knew that faith without works is dead and so I encouraged her to work hard during her therapy and stood with her each step of the way.

When she was wary, I stepped in to assist. My family rallied around her to support her in her recovery.

Even though I was afraid to lose my mom, I never allowed her to see that fear.

When our loved ones are sick and facing death, it forces us to face our own mortality.

We recognize that we are not invincible and that one day, we too will battle for our lives.

Have you been there; scared to lose someone you loved?

This is usually a time when we can question our God and our faith can waiver.

My faith in God grew during this time though. I relied on God to help my mom but to also help me through this frightening time.

My faith in God also grew during the times I worked with my mentor.

As I completed the activities he gave me; the introspection and reflection exercises, I realized that God had been my protector during even the most difficult of my circumstances.

As I worked through my challenges, faced my fears, and overcame my emotional issues, I relied on my relationship with God to sustain me when I felt any anxiety.

I realized and accepted that Romans 8:28 was true. I believed that "for those who love God all things work together for good, for those who are called according to his purpose."

I knew that I loved God and that I was called to fulfill his purpose.

As I had faith that my life experiences had purpose, I knew that my mom's life had purpose as well.

She had faith that her life would be used to help others. Not only did she have faith that her bad experiences with cancer would be a blessing, she took action.

She formed a cancer support group for women fighting various forms of cancer and worked with the group to inspire, motivate, and encourage them to be warriors and to stand as their sisters' keeper.

As head of the support group my mom worked with different organizations and entities to provide funding to support survivors in need and to ensure they have social outlets by hosting them to quarterly social events.

My faith in God has always paid off. I believe and have faith that God's purpose for my life will supersede every experience I have.

With this faith, I can walk through the fire knowing that all things will work for my benefit. This same belief is also available to you.

Faith is the "substance of things hoped for and the evidence of things not seen."

God responds to our acts of faith. Faith without work is dead. Even with faith, we must act.

Tips for increasing faith:

   1. ***Trust the process of life***

   2. ***Pray and meditate***

   3. ***Read scripture versus. Know the promises of God.***

4. Bounce back from your experiences with the lessons and rebuild stronger.

5. Believe in God's word.

6. Believe in yourself as a divine creation powered by the Divine Himself.

7. Trust the process of life.

After reading today's entry, I realize:

Today I want to focus and work on:

Today's affirmation:

I have faith that everything that has happened or will happen in my life has purpose.

I have faith that God is guiding my life.

Because I have faith, I will free myself from worry, anxiety, and turmoil.

I know that all things work together for good for those who love God and who are called according to His purpose.

I know that if I have just mustard seed faith, I can move mountains.

I have faith that my life will be a blessing to others.

I have faith in me.

I am fierce. I am brilliant. I am beautiful. I am amazing. I am an overcomer. I am a Queen.

When are you most resistant to when it comes to building your faith?

Of the items you were most resistant to, which can you work on?

Day 17 - Love

After all the broken relationships I had experienced, and the betrayal by the men I loved, I never thought the love I desired would manifest itself.

Love was just a fad.

Love was for people who believed in fairy tales.

As little girls, we read books and watched movies where women found their knights in shining armor and where the prince rescued the distressed maiden.

We are pressed in our twenties to be romantically involved, by thirty to be married and to have children.

Love songs that flood the air waves sing about undying love and romance while tugging at your heart.

The reality is society puts a tremendous amount of pressure on the single woman.

I have been in love one or two times and to be honest with you love was just painful.

It is about taking the risk to intimately learn someone while also exposing your vulnerabilities, desires, and dreams.

Love is about compromising on what you want for someone else's benefit.

It is about accepting someone else's faults. It is about tolerating bad moods, differences of opinions and selfishness.

Love is about sharing your world with someone who you hope will not abuse their access to you.

From very early in our lives, we are groomed to believe that we need to be in relationships.

As a result of this, our self-worth is attached to being involved in a romantic relationship.

We go from relationship to relationship seeking someone to complete us and to love us.

How many toxic or poor relationships did you endure all for the sake of being loved?

Now, in retrospect, as I inspected my love relationships, I realized that most of my love relationships were not the greatest partnerships.

In all honesty, most of them were painful but I continued to seek someone to "complete" me and to fulfill me.

I had put lots of energy into ensuring my partners were comfortable, happy, and secure in our relationship.

I had given up things I wanted, compromised when I did not want to, been disappointed when the effort was not reciprocal and broken when the relationship did not last.

I had put a lot of effort into being a part of something and loving someone else.

I needed to love myself. I needed to put the same energy into loving me that I had put into loving other people and I needed to establish boundaries to avoid being taken advantage of.

I also needed to stop looking at the world with jaded eyes; seeing only what I wanted to see versus what was real.

This realization did not happen until I finally took the time to understand why I allowed myself to be involved with a married man albeit unknown to me. He was the most deceitful person I have ever met.

I realized that, I needed to invest time into loving myself.